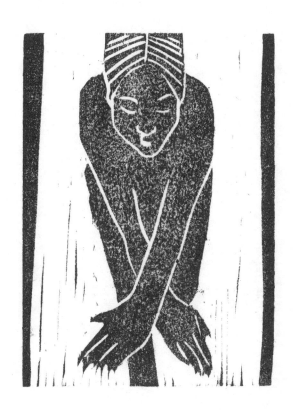

ORIGINAL SELF

LIVING WITH PARADOX AND AUTHENTICITY

Thomas Moore

Illustrated by Joan Hanley

 HarperCollins*Publishers*

To Joe and Pat and Ben and Mary

HarperCollins books may be purchased for educational,
business, or sales promotional use. For information please write:
Special Markets Department, HarperCollins Publishers Inc.,
10 East 53rd Street, New York, NY 10022.

FIRST EDITION

Designed by David Bullen

Printed on acid-free paper

ISBN 0-06-019542-8

00 01 02 03 04 ❖/RRD 10 9 8 7 6 5 4 3 2 1

PREFACE

Far beneath the many thick layers of indoctrination about who we are and who we should be lies an original self, a person who came into this world full of possibility and destined for joyful unveiling and manifestation. It is this person we glimpse in another when we fall in love or when we idealize a leader or romanticize an artist. This is the person who comes to life in us briefly as we get married, start a course in school, or try on a new job—before worry and cynicism have set in. Chronically trying to be someone other than this original self, persuaded that we are not adequate and should fit some norm of health or correctness, we may find a cool distance gradually separating us from that deep and eternal person, that God-given personality, and we may forget both who we were and who we might be.

I began *Care of the Soul* by saying that all of our problems, personal and social, are due to a loss of soul. The truth of that statement becomes clearer as every day passes and history continues to multiply its tragedies. But I have also come to see that soul is lost in our everyday lives whenever we try to force ourselves to fit some norm of health or correctness. When the ever-creative soul is allowed to rise up from the deep reservoir of life that is its home, we become unpredictable and not easily squeezed into narrow expectations of what a person should be. In the flush of the soul's vitality, we become eccentric. Our creative madness, the constructive kind that Plato discussed, gives our lives a shape that we could never plan or design.

The small pieces in this book together offer a comprehensive portrait of an alternative kind of person, one who lives from the burning core of the heart, with the creativity that comes from allowing the soul to blossom in its own colors and shapes. The book is like a kaleidoscope. Turning a page is like tilting the colored glass into yet another pattern. And each idea and image reflects yet another way we become an individual by following the lead of the soul.

As I imagine it, if we suppress this deep vitality and lose touch with our original self, we might well fall into a depression that is not just personal but that reflects the failure of this society, for all its praise of the individual, to nurture and support the wide-ranging possibilities of a human life. In many subtle ways—in education, politics, economics, and at work—we demand that men and women trade in their desire and joy for economic success and social approval, and thus we spread the depression that is the characteristic emotional malady of our time. Of course, society is us, and rediscovering our original selves means finding ourselves through service and compassion to others. We might also learn how to support others as they look for signs of their originality and experiment with it.

One important aspect of finding one's original core is the realization that the deeper one goes into the self, the more poetic one's language and ideas become. It is appropriate that this book be one of visual images as well as ideas. Joan Hanley's woodcuts attempt to divine the archetype in each piece. These images are not really illustrative of the ideas; rather they evoke the mystery in their own way, so that each page is a duet played by writer and artist. Each image also intensifies the idea, allowing us to meditate on it in another way. Each image interprets the writing and dreams the dream onward, elucidating without suggesting an end to wonder.

The original self is a seed of wondrous possibility and reeks with pleasure. One hopes that the special form of this book will offer pleasure to the reader with its brevity, its variety, the dialogue between quoted authors and myself, and the visual appeal of the pages. My wish is to have created a book one wants to carry around and keep at hand, a book that will move from friend to friend and belong in a personal library.

In my own experience, it is often the brief, simple, original books that turn out to be the most useful. The books I have on my special shelf—books for personal, lifelong use—are all brief and untraditionally structured. They are almost all illustrated, and they have considerable blank space on a page. These are not sources of information but books for meditation. A book is virtual space that invites contemplation and perusal. In this space one tarries and looks around, absorbing the atmosphere, and then leaves, the author hopes, happy to have visited.

The Taoist master Nü-yü was once asked, "Sir, you are advanced in years,
and yet you still have the face of a child. What can be the
secret? Said Nü-yü, "I have been instructed in the Tao."

Chuang Tzu

Be mindful of all your daily matters, then you'll be just living
with unborn Buddha-mind. Originally, no one is deluded.

Bankei Yotaku

Original Self

What was the purpose of his pilgrimage?
To make a new intelligence prevail.
Wallace Stevens, "The Comedian as the Letter C"

Oᴜʀ ᴏᴅʏssᴇʏ ᴏғ sᴏᴜʟ ʀᴜɴs ɪɴ ᴄᴏᴜɴᴛᴇʀᴘᴏɪɴᴛ
ᴛᴏ ᴏᴜʀ ᴏᴅʏssᴇʏ ᴏғ ʟɪғᴇ.

Odyssey is a noble image for the mysterious process we call a human life. At the very font of our civilization we are fortunate to have Homer's tale of the travels of the antihero Odysseus. His is a sacred story, not the account of man on the literal seas trying to get home, but the mystery drama of Everyman, the deep story of us all, men and women, as we try to make our way through life with the hope of arriving at a place that can be called home.

This journey is a soul voyage. Odysseus encounters many fantastic creatures and people, and makes a visit to the realm of the dead as well, all part of his journey of homecoming. Each of us is on such a journey, embracing both the concrete situation of our lives and an inner pilgrimage as well. We have to work out the details of our lives, but at the same time we are challenged to deal with the past, the world the dead have made for us, and the deep inner life that is under and beyond the literal events that absorb our attention.

Our age seems obstinately focused on the external details of this journey, and autobiographies and biographies tend to dwell on the facts of a life. There are remarkable exceptions, of course, like C. G. Jung's *Memories, Dreams, Reflections*, which is the story of a soul, but generally we try to make sense of life by constructing it outwardly to fit external criteria and expectations.

As we ignore the inner life, or at least the symbolic life expressed in the poetry of our actions and the events of our lives, the inner world doesn't vanish; in our neglect it gathers strength as it continues to influence us. But unfamiliar with its ways, we are in large measure cut off from its progress. We sense its ups and downs in moods and emotions that seem to have little connection to life, but we try to control those vague sensations with medication and manipulation rather than make specific adjustments in response to their meaning.

The soul has its own set of rules, which are not the same as those of life. Unlike the steady progress of history, for instance, the events of the soul are cyclic and repetitive. Familiar themes come round and round. The past is more important than the future. The living and the dead have equal roles. Emotions and the sense of meaning are paramount. Pleasures are deep, and pain can reach the very foundations of our existence.

Without becoming mystics, we could become more closely acquainted with the ways of the inner life. If they are noted and taken seriously, dreams can turn our attention downward and inward and give clues to the dynamics of the heart and the imagination. Moods, attitudes, influences, aspirations, and fears also ask for a degree of sophistication in our response. We could contemplate them, discuss them, and educate ourselves in their intricacies and vagaries.

Today many people live the external life exclusively, and when the inner world erupts or stirs, they rush to a therapist or druggist for help. They try to explain profound mythic developments in the language of behavior and experience. Often they have no idea what is happening to them, because they have been so cut off from the deep self. Their own soul is so alien to them that they are unaware of what is going on outside the known realm of fact.

Former methods of keeping in touch with the inner life have gone out of mode. Diaries, letters, and deep conversations help focus attention on developments and materials that lie beneath the surface. Only one hundred years ago, without benefit of typewriters and word processors, people kept elaborate, long, and detailed diaries and notebooks. We seem to have left behind these methods of reflection in favor of technologies for action.

Poetry and serious literature can also offer guidance. A small amount of good literature can often teach more about the inner life than volumes of psychology. The ancient literatures of many traditions offer insight into the inner life. They can teach us how to sketch out a spiritual autobiography instead of a résumé of skills and facts. They also show that we are on an odyssey and that the people who enter our lives and the events that take place have deep significance, often symbolic and imagistic.

The soul doesn't evolve or grow, it cycles and twists, repeats and reprises, echoing ancient themes common to all human beings. It is always circling home. Gnostic tales tell of the homesickness of the soul, its yearning for its own milieu, which is not this world of fact. Its odyssey is a drifting at sea, a floating toward home, not an evolution toward perfection.

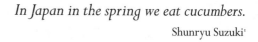

In Japan in the spring we eat cucumbers.
Shunryu Suzuki[1]

Honor the seasons of nature and the rhythms of your life.

The Zen master Shunryu Suzuki-Roshi, former abbot of Tassajara monastery in California, ends his remarkable book, *Zen Mind, Beginner's Mind,* with the advice to live as though nothing exists except momentarily in its present form. We should remain attached to nothing, he says, not even to our philosophy of life or our spiritual path. Better to be present to what is happening than to be lost in our ideas and beliefs.

In the most ordinary ways, we have lost the guidance of nature to live in accord with the rhythms and cycles of the soul. We eat food that is out of season, and we even change our clocks to keep the dark at bay by extending the light of summer. Accustomed to control, we forget that our physical and emotional life is musical, with all sorts of sensations, fantasies, and feelings coming and going like the flighty motifs of fugues, sonatas, and canons.

Estranged from the music of our own lives, we endure our ordinary days with existential anxiety. We worry about the past and anticipate the future, all the while overlooking the season of the moment. If we were to embrace the past without excessive judgment and calmly step, not leap, into the future, we might feel the vitality of the all-embracing soul.

Being present to the life that presses upon us does not mean simply being alert and full of consciousness. Surrendering to a daydream or a memory may be a way of being engaged with the present. Drifting into reverie might bring us to the full immediacy of the moment, which may be properly focused on invisible things. Turned inward, we might be completely present, and conversely, being wide awake to life might be a distraction and, to the soul, a kind of sleep.

The principle of being present to life is also complicated by the soul's odd sense of time, so different from the literal measurements of the clock and calendar. The soul exists in cycles of time, full of repetition, and it has equal portions of flowing temporality and static eternity. Responsive to the soul, we may easily drift out of literal life several times a day to revisit people and places of the past or to imagine the future. These visitations are entirely different from the ego's anxious attempts to resolve the past or control the future. They are more like a summer's week on a beach, a way to get away and find a fresh perspective.

Living in the moment can become a moralistic principle, a burden rather than a way to intensify life. The difference might depend on who takes the lead in the dance and who chooses the music. The soul is a community of many interior persons, many of them capable leaders. The ego is only one among them and probably should not always run the show. A good dancer or musician allows the music to take over, becomes absorbed in the complex harmonies and tempos, and is the servant of the materials at hand. The secret of a soul-based life is to allow someone or something other than the usual self to be in charge.

Looking for guidance, wisely we may prevail upon a friend or a professional counselor, or we may consult our dreams and ideas. An alternative is to pay close heed to the natural seasons, letting go of some of the control over our actions, allowing an external principle, more beneath the ego than above it, to set the pace. We are nature, and to be profoundly in synch with the seasons and the weather is an effective way to be in tune with our deeper selves. Obeying the sun, regarding the moon, imitating the plants, moving with the winds, we find that elusive sense of self that we thought was only interior and not part of the world.

Our fruits educate us and fit us to live here in New England. Better for us is the wild strawberry than the pine-apple, the wild apple than the orange, the chestnut and pignut than the cocoa-nut and almond, and not on account of their flavor merely, but the part they play in our education.

Henry David Thoreau[2]

LIVE SIMPLY, BUT BE COMPLICATED.

Simplifying life is a route to mindfulness, but simplicity can easily be sentimentalized. Inspired by such a philosophy, a person might build a log cabin in the woods and yet find that life was still not simple. Simplicity of soul is not necessarily the same as simplicity of life, and certainly not the same as simplicity of character and personality. When Henry David Thoreau simplified his life at Walden Pond, as his writings of that time show, his interior life became more complicated. As Emerson said in his elegy for his friend, emotionally he was not a simple man: "There was somewhat military in his nature, not to be subdued, always manly and able, but rarely tender, as if he did not feel himself except in opposition."[3]

Simplifying the externals allows us to cultivate a rich inner and outer life. A cluttered existence may keep us busy, but busyness doesn't mean that we are fully engaged in what we are doing. Usually, just the opposite, we feel busy because we are neurotically active at things that don't matter much in the long run. It does little good to be successful in a business that requires sixty hours of work a week, while the simple pleasures of home life are neglected. A complicated person can simplify life and in that simplicity find a sharp articulation of values. Complicated lives often do the opposite: they show to what extent the person is lost in the busyness of the world.

Sometimes we may make a dramatic improvement in daily living by making a surgically precise excision from our daily affairs. For many, turning off the television would be an act of simplifying that might have magical results. For me, staying home works magic, when worldly wisdom recommends travel. Not buying something, not going somewhere, and not watching something can each be an effective application of the simplicity rule.

Living closer to nature helps simplify because nature itself, though complex, keeps us in tune with basic rhythms and pleasures that never change and that provide grounding. When our family moved next to a farm, we found simplicity in the food we ate and in new sources for our entertainment and pleasure. Learning how to ride a horse is a complicated process, but riding is a simple pleasure that offers lasting satisfaction.

As Thoreau says, our local fruits can educate us and show us how to live. Living close to our natural world, in tune with its seasons and its peculiarities, we find a simplicity of life. We live in a real place that is our own, and we belong to it. Exotic deviations are enriching—an Italian restaurant, an Asian grocery, an African clothing store—but these require a base in life determined by the character of our landscape, our animals and birds, and our trees and plants. Living simply where we are, we stay physically healthy and find emotional security.

Prudence is an old maid courted by incapacity.
William Blake, "Proverbs of Hell"

BEING SMART ABOUT LIFE LEADS US DOWN A SUPERIOR
BUT NARROW ROAD OF SELF-DECEPTION.

In our modern existential anxiety, we worry that we may not know ourselves, that we may not fully understand nature, or that our children may grow up without the skills they need to be successful. We feel compelled to read the popular book of the moment and to find an extraordinary teacher or a worthy school of thought. We place our hopes in new theories and technologies of learning, the more electronically pyrotechnic the better. And yet these days we seem unable to accomplish the basic necessities—remain married, raise tranquil children, live in safe neighborhoods, and find happiness at work.

We want so badly to do the right thing, and yet religions have taught for millennia that we are fundamentally ignorant about the nature of things. We pride ourselves on our freshly won intelligence, while religion teaches the value of holy ignorance. There is a thickheaded form of not knowing, from not having reflected or thought, and an inspired way, being sufficiently educated that we realize how absurdly little we know. The former is plain ignorance, the latter verges on the sacred.

If we are not always smart about the choices we make, we may allow our decisions to rise from a deeper place, a place lower than rational intelligence. Sure guidance in life may come from sources that are inimical to intelligence: such things as desire, interest, fear, intuition, fantasy, inclination, and even divination. We may make better choices not knowing what we are doing than deluding ourselves by thinking that we are aware and intelligent.

Of course, however bright or dim we are, we will still make mistakes. If I kept a diary of all the bad decisions I have made in my life, it would be too thick to carry. But as in most things, it may take a bundle of mistakes to arrive at something sublime, just as it takes thousands of flowers to produce a few drops of perfume.

In fact, prudence may often be little more than a defense against making mistakes. Especially if we are trying self-consciously to be prudent, the very thought of wisdom could well be educed as an effective reason for not allowing life to take its course. Doing the prudent thing may prevent us from following our passions. It may overrun our intuitions and may give us the illusion of being virtuous when life is asking us to explore territory lying beneath the horizon of virtue.

It is a short step, as it was in the history of the word, from prudence to prudery. To be a prude is to sentimentalize our acumen, cutting away its shadow. Jane Austin contrasts prudence with romance; others might think of it as the opposite of foolishness. I imagine prudence as the antipode of passion, a pale aura of anxiety keeping us at a healthy distance from the blood soul.

The word means "to look ahead," an image that contains some warnings about being prudent. Maybe we shouldn't look too far ahead and miss what is presently before us, and maybe we should look at everything that is ahead, not only what we wish would be there. Anxiety is nothing but fear inspired by an imagined future collapse. It is the failure of trust.

A good tonic for runaway prudence is wisdom, though wisdom, too, can shine too brightly. Generally, if we follow the prudent path, we will live in the land of one-sided virtue, where difficulties abound. But if we can find some wisdom, we will not limit our actions to what seems prudent at the expense of romance, passion, and occasional folly.

Our emotional symptoms, neurotic habits, and life problems are precious sources of life and individuality.

To be modern is to worship at the altar of health. We look forward to the day when we will be fully balanced and adjusted. We believe we will have arrived there when trouble vanishes and we feel chronically carefree.

This reasonable assumption compels many to read self-help books and to trust in psychotherapy. It accounts for our enshrinement of medicine and for the therapeutic philosophy that characterizes the modern mind. We are hell-bent on being healthy and on fixing anything and everything that appears broken, including a broken life.

Behind this attitude lies a salvational fantasy, the hope that we may be saved from those aspects of human life that seem unfortunate and remain an obstacle to the carefree existence we see in our daydreams. The trouble with this attitude is that the healthier we feel, the less reflective we become, the more our sense of reality zooms into the ether and our humanity recedes.

When I look back on my life, I see a long train of mistakes and failures.

Remembering them is painful, and I hope I don't have to endure many more of them. Yet I can also see how each of those failures helped to shape me and my life, such as it is. Later pleasures required earlier pain, and the creative, happy elements in my life now would not exist without the grace of former failures.

I don't mean to criticize the desire for happiness, but only to point out that it has a companion—the necessity of suffering. Put these two together and we have a complete view of life, one carved out of blissful desires and painful failures. I don't look for a midpoint where all is in order. Such a delicate balance would be flat and pallid. I don't expect the pleasures to offset the sorrows. Each independently, in unequal measure, offers vitality.

Patricia Berry's specific contribution is to help us see that our symptoms point toward the future and promise a transformation of failure into form. I have always been shy and reserved—an embarrassing weakness I try to cover up. I have been criticized for it, and all my life people have encouraged me to be different. Indeed, in recent years strangers have offered many suggestions for my improvement. But although I would enjoy a cure for this malady, I am attached to it. It helps me work. I seem able to absorb failures and have no need to provide answers for the many questions that appear before me. Some may take this application of my personal shyness as a fault, but I see some positive outcomes.

I remember once in a group discussion James Hillman was celebrating the soul's pathologies. I supported his stance by saying how important it is to safeguard our symptoms. A man in the group came up to me afterward and said, "Did I hear you right? Did you speak in favor of preserving our symptoms? How could a therapist, of all people, make such an odd remark?"

Our neuroses are the raw material out of which an interesting personality may be crafted. They are sometimes dangerous and debilitating but nonetheless valuable. They are the basic stuff of the soul in need of lifelong refinement. Working this annoying and embarrassing material for a lifetime is a realistic work compared with the search for psychological hygiene—ridding ourselves of failure and confusion.

Not wallowing in our limitations but creatively dealing with them as resources for a vital life—the *prima materia* of the alchemists—we arrive not at shallow self-acceptance but at profound love of the soul, which, with its rich mixture of the good and the bad, is the starting point of a creative life.

"To give yourself fully is a beautiful and thrilling privilege"
[said Professor Mephesto, quoting Candy].
Terry Southern and Mason Hoffenberg[5]

Naïveté and cynicism mark the failure to achieve innocence.

To live an ethical life and to feel comfortable with oneself, it is necessary to achieve a degree of innocence. But we sometimes confuse naïveté and innocence. We may think it is mature to be cynical and immature to be innocent. But most of us need to feel liberated from the weight of heavy karma, free of guilt, and in some way guileless in the eyes of the world. There is a kind of innocence that is both intelligent and worldly-wise.

Naïveté is the failure to grow up and enter adult life. Americans are naive in many ways, sometimes identifying with noble values while acting out in outrageously self-serving and violent ways. We seem to believe in our naive values and fail to see the defining contradiction of our culture: our noble ideals joined to the atrocious ways we often treat ourselves and the people of the world. Our naïveté blinds us to our actual values and to the disasters we inflict.

This is not to say that we are all villains or that we do no good, but we are deluded by an "innocence complex," a false self-image that is cleaner than the one the facts show. We believe ourselves to be innocent, and yet in every sphere we act corruptly. In many cultures, corruption is an art. But we want to have it both ways: we want a clear conscience and the freedom to act deviously. The result is not only to confuse those from other cultures who have to deal with us, but in the depths of our hearts, to deprive us of the genuine innocence we need.

Confusion about innocence has disastrous effects on our behavior and attitudes. If we don't feel innocent, we may give in to cynicism, and then all values become irrelevant. We may not even try to conduct business ethically; we may feel no compunction in harming others. The absence of innocence may contribute to a collapse of values.

We are born naive, but we can grow into innocence, which is something to be achieved. On the way toward innocence, we may pass through stages where we feel guilty or even dally with evil—pusillanimous souls do not find innocence easily. With courage we may gain enough acquaintance with real life to make choices that foster our innocence while avoiding naïveté or cynicism.

My mentors in archetypal psychology used to talk about split archetypes. When a certain constructive life pattern fails, it often divides into two extreme and destructive variations. When strength falters, for example, the breakdown may show itself as excessive vulnerability on one side and extreme aggressiveness on the other. In a similar way, failed innocence may split into naïveté and cynicism.

When innocence is so divided, its symptomatic forms may alternate within a person or a group. One may be naive one moment and cynical the next. A sense of purity may cover over actions that are full of guilt. Or one person or group may become the cynical aggressor and the other the naive victim. In all cases, the soul is kept out by these thick, blind complexes. In such a condition one may feel driven, out of control, or just plain ignorant.

In alchemy, after a long and difficult process of sorting and uniting, a white bird is pictured flying out of the retort of transformation. This bird may be seen as the innocence that is achieved after a long struggle with temptations toward corruption. This kind of innocence arrives only late in the process, after much toil and experiment. It is hard-won, but it is a sign of the soul's evolution.

Innocence, won only after years of struggle toward a deeply ethical life in a culture torn between naive ideals and cynical behavior, allows one to accept oneself absolutely: to forgive oneself for past ignorance and stupidity and to breathe the invigorating air of qualified purity.

*See how widely I have ranged, Lord, searching for you in
my memory. I have not found you outside it.*

Saint Augustine[6]

CONTEMPLATIVELY REMEMBERING THE PAST NURTURES THE SOUL.

I have two remarkable memories of remembering. One is the example of my
Uncle Tom, a farmer, who in my childhood told me countless stories of neighbors and family. It was as though he lived for memories, which he recounted
to me with great wit and pleasure during work hours and after and before.

The second is my experience as a psychotherapist. In the long hours of therapy, people told stories of their childhood, almost always searching for a clue
to their adult emotional suffering. Their resort to memory was not pure. It was
not for the sake of memory itself and certainly not for the pleasure of remembering, as in the case of my Uncle Tom.

In therapy I tried hard to receive memories for their own sake, but given the
psychological climate of our times, it was not easy to avoid the exploitation of
memory as a therapeutic resource. I saw remembering as a way of leaving the
present practical world for the realm of the soul. I felt instructed by the Neoplatonic philosophers of old who saw such excursions as valuable in their own
right. You don't have to do anything with memories, but only have them.

When a thing can't be remembered, it may be that we fear the implications of the memory, and so when we dare to allow the memory, we invite a cutoff piece of life and self to come back into view. Now we may have the courage to recall, and in the process a gaping sore may be sutured by the simple threads of memory.

In a long passage on memory in his *Confessions*, Saint Augustine says that we understand everything in relation to what we have remembered. Memory gives us not only personal remembrances of events but also archetypal images, a memory not only of things that were but also of things that always are. By calling to mind the various ways in which human life can be lived, we broaden and deepen our imagination, and life opens up to us.

Memory requires certain arts that cultivate it and tease out its many variations and possibilities. Telling stories from childhood or simply from the past brings memory into play. A certain kind of meditation might activate memory, and what may seem to be distractions during meditation—the insistence of memories—may be just what is needed. The memories that pop up spontaneously during a moment of absorption nurture the imagination and educate the emotions.

Dreams often contain memories or at least suggest events of the past. Perhaps therapy is of value precisely because it is one of the few areas in life that honors memory. Photography has profoundly affected modern memory, and even in simple home settings an album of photos may be important to the soul as a source of memories. Keeping old buildings and objects also gives memory a vivid place in ordinary life and adds immeasurably to the soul of a place.

It is easy to dismiss a memory that slips into view, thinking it unimportant. But just remarking on it, mentioning it to a friend, even noting it yourself, gives it the slightest honor. We might just recite the memory, however fragmentary, and not give in to the idle curiosity involved in trying to make sense of it.

Memory holds us together as individuals and as communities. When we forget who we have been, we lose a full sense of who we are. People who have drifted apart from the soul or who want to defend themselves against the pain of experience often make an effort to erase memories. They move away from the actual scene of pain, tear down buildings associated with tragedy, or at a personal level, they get as busy as possible so that memory won't have a chance to penetrate their consciousness.

Memory is potent. It does something to us. It makes us who we are. It gives us depth. It ties our past to our present to overcome the disjunction of a too literal life. It focuses our attention on the imagination of events rather than on events taken literally. Memory is a kind of poetry.

"Help yourself to the food and welcome, and then afterward, when you have tasted dinner, we shall ask you who among men you are."

Odyssey 4.60[7]

Welcome the Other into your life, both the stranger and the strange.

When a society loses its soul, it develops many neurotic behaviors, among them paranoia and xenophobia. Xenophobia is anxiety in the presence of strangers or simply whatever is strange and unusual. The *Odyssey* is a story about a wandering man who is always a stranger among those he visits on his journey. The Greeks were well aware of the vulnerability of the traveler and considered it a great virtue to offer hospitality.

We are each *Homo viator,* each on a unique odyssey. We are all vulnerable on our journey and need the hospitality and understanding of others. But it takes an awakened heart to identify with others through our own needs and experiences. When the heart goes numb, as it does when a culture loses its soul in a generic way, we can no longer feel empathy based on our own emotions. We may feel cold and lonely in a world where deep hospitality has disappeared, and on the other hand, we may close our hearts to the needs of others because we have lost the capacity for empathy.

Empathy is the work of the imagination, the ability to recognize the impact (the *pathos* in em-pathy) of life upon another. We may not have the capacity for empathy because our attention is fixed on ourselves and cannot make the shift toward another. Anxiety about our own welfare may preclude the very imagination of another's distress. As with any manifestation of narcissism, it doesn't help to encourage altruism, because the root problem is a failure to care enough about ourselves.

A first step toward empathy might seem paradoxical: we may have to discover our own worth and have a basis for self-concern. It is impossible to appreciate the complexity of others if we are not able to love ourselves, knowing our contradictions. A positive love for one's own soul then might extend beyond oneself to include the world, and it might have more emotional weight than an abstract tolerance for humankind.

It is not enough to let down our defenses and overcome our xenophobia. An awakened soul requires more of us: not just an end to xenophobia, but the development of positive xenophilia—love of strangers and the unusual, an appreciation for cultures that are unlike our own, and a desire to know groups and individuals that have different ways of understanding and living. All that is not ego is by nature exotic, outside the familiar and usually protected and defended precinct of the self, and so, as we awaken to a life beyond egotistic narcissism, we might feel an attraction to the unfamiliar.

When we are living only a portion of what a human being is capable of, our lives are incomplete. I don't mean that we each have to do everything possible in life, but that the more possibilities we can imagine, the richer our lives will be. Defending ourselves against the stranger is a way of keeping out our own potentiality. The diminishment of our acquaintances is a diminishment of ourselves.

The most challenging stranger is life itself, or the soul, the face and source of vitality. Life is always presenting new possibilities, and we may fear that bountifulness. It may seem safer to be content with what we have and what we are, and so we cling to the status quo. But in these matters there is no convenient plateau. When we refuse a new offering of life, we develop emotional calluses. The habit of acting from fear sets in quickly and becomes steadily more rigid. Refusing life, we become attendants of death.

Therefore we need arts of xenophilia, constructive and habitual ways of welcoming the unfamiliar. One concrete way is to travel with an open mind, not judging others by what you already know and love, but being receptive to alternative ways of imagining the good life. Xenophilia may involve nothing more challenging than eating or even cooking unfamiliar food, learning another language, wearing some clothes of another culture, reading about and from other societies, or making an effort to become acquainted with people from distant lands. All of these things may be done for business or for information and education, but they have a different flavor when they are done from the heart, with no gain in sight except the personal pleasure of enlarging one's imagination.

Almost every day we are asked to extend the range of our acquaintance with life. It is one of several ways to live intensely, and it is also a way to prepare for death. For death is the ultimate stranger. This is not necessarily a morbid thought, because only by allowing death to play a role in daily life do we really live. Opening to another society or another individual—they are two levels of culture—we die a little death in relation to what has become familiar. But those little deaths create openings to new life.

Lɪꜰᴇ ɴᴇᴇᴅꜱ ᴀ ᴘᴏɪɴᴛ ᴏꜰ ᴇɴᴛʀʏ, ᴀ ᴄʀᴀᴄᴋ ɪɴ ᴏᴜʀ ᴅᴇꜰᴇɴꜱᴇꜱ.

In therapy I often heard variations on the dream of an unlocked gate or a door ajar. The dreamer was usually afraid, vulnerable to and undefended against an imagined unknown intruder. I could empathize with the dreamer. I sense the anxiety in my own life when I have neglected to shield myself from the impact of another person or from emotions that could alter my life. The status quo is a treasured thing and calls for protection. But an established habit of defensiveness is not the same as defending oneself in the presence of a threat. The former is a neurotic habit, while the latter is a way of keeping sane.

Life is a lover who wants us for himself. Tradition says that as Eros he may have the chubby face of an angelic cherub or an attractive if unruly adolescent. In either case his wings are large, and with them he lifts us up and inspires enthusiasm. But he also works in tandem with death and marks the demise of the treasured status quo. No wonder we feel two ways about life: we want to invite it in, but sometimes we would rather keep it out.

26

The door ajar is yet another image for the unheroic work of caring for the soul. It is not a project, as is the job of personal growth or self-improvement. It is not so much something we do as it is something done to us. Our role is to stand out of the way or allow a point of entry. It is helpful to learn how to defend oneself so as not to be undone entirely by the course of feelings and the copious possibilities of love and life, but we don't have to seal ourselves off altogether. We need only keep the door unlocked or allow a window to remain undone a crack.

Pope John XXIII used a powerful and relevant image when he convoked his Vatican Council. "*Apriamo le finestre*" (Let's open the windows), he said. When he suggested that the locks be loosened and the catches released, fear arose among the church hierarchy. What would happen? What new ideas might enter?

In these door-ajar dreams, the dreamer often thinks he has slipped up. Usually he keeps the doors shut and the windows secure, but somehow they have come undone. Has he forgotten? Has someone else released them? Is something mischievous or threatening going on?

The dreamer often assumes that a thief will break in. The dream often has a strong Hermes tone. Who is outside, thinking of coming in? Not a friend. Whoever it is plans some kind of breaking and entering. It is a thief, who in dreams is always Hermes stealing what is most precious. Hermes guides the soul—his classical duty—by taking away the very thing we most want but do not need.

But right here is another odd aspect of the soul's progress. It is created more by loss than by gain. One forgets, and life enters. One doesn't understand, and life increases. One experiences the loss of health or a loved one, and mysteriously life takes a promising course.

In order to have soul, we need to be taken from, and that necessary empty-ing requires some collusion on our part in the theft, some neglect in our defenses, some distraction that interferes with our intentions. It won't do to make a project of keeping the door ajar. It has to come from a distracted mind, one that is not so excessively preoccupied with defending itself that theft is not possible.

Puer natus est nobis.
Introit, Catholic Mass

T HE FOUNTAIN OF YOUTH IS REAL,
BUT MORE SUBTLE THAN WE IMAGINE IT.

In the Christian tradition the midnight Mass at Christmas begins with the song "A child is born to us." The Latin for *child* here is *puer,* a word often used by the ancient Romans to describe a youth and used later by C. G. Jung to name the spirit of youth that is an essential part of us all.

Puer is not simply literal young age, but an attitude of youthfulness that may be full of spirit, ambition, high destiny, and a forgetfulness of mortality. It is a spirit that brings new life, and it isn't far-fetched to understand Christmas as the celebration of this eternal spirit or to see it in the new year pictured appropriately as a baby decked out in a diaper. As Jung says, dreams of children may signal some new beginning, a fresh turning of the cycle.

In psychology puer also refers to a type of man or woman who embodies this idealistic, romantic, playful, and self-contained spirit, or in whom this spirit is dominant and defining. In Jungian terms, puer is an aspect of the animus, a spirit that characterizes both men and women. Some people seem to retain their youthful spirit far into old age and maybe for the length of their lives. In others it is a spirit that comes and goes.

The puer spirit is both a blessing and a curse. It can fill people with optimism and energy and keep them feeling and even looking young. My father is now in his mid-eighties, and he has always had a strong puer in him, although it has also always been seasoned with old man qualities, which he had even in his youth. He seems eternally in love with life and at eighty-six is embarking on new life endeavors.

I sense the puer in me in both creative and inhibiting ways. I have aimed high all my life, from the day I left home at thirteen to begin a long, ultimately unfulfilled education toward the Catholic priesthood. I never feel far removed from my boyhood, and I have a deep romanticism about art and life that is one sign of a kind of puer. On the other hand, I feel strongly that a part of me wants never to grow up, and never does. I don't know the ways of the world well, and I am quite unrealistic about many basic aspects of life.

The puer is an aspect of the spiritual side of a man or woman rather than the deep, downward, grounded soul. The puer spirit keeps us moving, looking ahead, creating and imagining. The puer spirit is well represented in high-tech industries, where it links up well with ever-changing technology and fast-moving calculations. A computer itself may be a puer object.

It is often difficult to pin down a puer, establish a friendship or a marriage, fit them snugly into an organization, or even get them to stay around for a while. The puer spirit may be completely unrealistic and unreliable, yet at the same time astonish with its unending fertile output of ideas and possibilities. To the puer, life may look more like a game than a serious business.

When the puer spirit shows up, it offers great promise. We may find the puer rising after a period of cool discontent or fallow wintering of the soul. Its appearance signals a renaissance of possibility, and yet it may be wise to tend the puer spirit cautiously, to find ways to connect it with the many other spirits that go together to make an interesting and creative human life. The puer is our creativity. It soars but doesn't necessarily foster our relationships or offer security and stability.

IT'S ALL RIGHT TO BE SAD.

When people of the Renaissance and Middle Ages referred to the depressed
state as being "in Saturn," they were suggesting that depression is a quality
of life and things. A tree may look depressed, or an animal. A building, too,
and a city may show its depression. The weather, of course, can be cheerful or
depressed—meteorologists talk about highs and lows, troughs and depres-
sions.

Perhaps the word *depression* is not the best one to describe the Saturnine side
of life because it has come to sound clinical, as if it's something we have, like
the measles, rather than a spirit, like Saturn, who is visiting or who has taken
up residence. On the other hand, the word *depressed* does suggest the weight
traditionally ascribed to Saturn, pressing us down and keeping us still.

Clinical psychologists often insist that depression is dangerous and is a physical symptom, a disease. Understandably they don't want it to be taken lightly,
as a simple passing mood, as though we were just having a bad day. People suf-

fer chronic depression bitterly, finding their work and relationships threatened. It can be at the root of delusions, paranoia, and other disorienting fantasies and can sometimes lead to suicide. Depression is serious, but its seriousness does not require that we reduce it to a physical malady, treat it exclusively with drugs, and thereby keep the soul out of it.

Depression wears many faces. It may induce withdrawal, solitude, sadness, heaviness, weariness, emptiness, coldness—a wide variety of feelings and attitudes. To enter depression creatively, it might be best to start by describing the feeling in the most ordinary and concrete terms. Simple, descriptive words would convey the *experience,* which we can address thoughtfully, whereas the clinical language invites a mechanical response and places us and our mood in a purely materialistic, dehumanizing context. For all its pain and dangers, depression can be humanizing, provided that we imagine it humanely.

People often say that there is no imagination in depression. It is a void, a dark pit, a cave with no exit. The more they look for a hint of meaning or some enlightening imagery, the more discouraged they become because it seems ever clearer that there is no value in it and no way out.

But our problem may be that we are not used to appreciating the particular kind of imagery proper to depression. The feeling of emptiness is itself a fantasy as well as an emotion. We could describe our despair, paint it, sketch it in a poem, as so many have done. We could be led directly by our hollow feelings to observe the hollowness of life, not only of our personal lives, but of the culture in which we live.

A portion of the suffering in depression comes from our inability to give it language and imagery. It feels vague and therefore without meaning. We don't know what to do because we don't know what it is. But if we could become better at articulating the imagery of despair and sadness, we might be that much closer to the meaning that would make it bearable. We may need a depressive aesthetics, an art of emptiness.

The next step might be to let the mood do its work. Depression is a daimonic visitation by a spirit that for centuries was described as remote, cold, abstract, and heavy. Generally our moods don't exactly come and go; they appear and subject us to a particular alchemy that transforms us, helps us deepen and develop. Their presence may be momentarily painful, but they always have a creative side that leaves a positive impression. Saturn was honored as the god of contemplation, religion, philosophy, and cool consideration. As Pico says, this spirit makes us contemplate. It takes our thoughts deep and far. There our thoughts are heavy because they bear so much meaning, even if at the same time they feel empty. Paradoxically, emptiness is one of the heaviest ideas in religion and philosophy.

In states of profound sadness we are carrying at least the weight of our lives, which may cry out for meaning, but we may be keeping our sadness at a distance by not giving it the space and welcome it requires. Sadness may creep in unawares day after day as life shows its intransigence and failure. Understandably we may be sad that the world is suffering so much. It's appropriate that we despair at the prospect of continuing brutal wars and hungry children. We seem to have a choice between deep sadness, which could move us to respond to the causes of sadness, and the existential and absolute pretense that this is the way it is, always was, and always will be. We carry the depression of life in our hearts, thinking that the weight must be personal, unaware that it is the world around us that is suffering. Not seeing the nature of our world's sadness, we feel its anonymity as a symptom of its presence.

The worst response to depression might be to translate it into self-pity, camouflaged as therapeutic work on our own sadness. The best response might be to respond courageously to the world's suffering. The attachment to sadness one sometimes senses in people diagnosed as depressed may simply be the odd presence of ego in what is the world's malady. If we could let go of the need to make it personal by clutching it close as a symptom, we might find some relief by discovering its proper milieu.

THE DETECTIVE MYSTERY IS A VERSION OF THE ULTIMATE
MYSTERY THAT DEFINES OUR DAYS.

What is the allure of the detective mystery, and what does it mean to detect a
mystery? We don't call detectives solvers, even though a decent fictional detective always solves the crime in the end. To detect is simply to notice, although
the root of the word is stronger, meaning to uncover.

The appeal of a detective story lies in the deeper mystery of life and death.
Do we have the intelligence and perspicacity to detect the mysteries at work in
our own lives? In the twentieth century in particular, the detective story has
been a favorite on television, on stage, and in the movies. But why should we
be so engaged with this form? Is it so rich, or does it appeal to something deep
and significant in our lives?

The Greeks referred to persons who had participated in the holy mysteries as *mystes* and believed they were exceptional and graced people. The Romans spoke of *mysterium* and connected it to the worship of gods and goddesses. In Marcel Detienne's extraordinary book, *The Masters of Truth in Archaic Greece*, he traces the meaning of the Greek word for truth, *aletheia*, which was sometimes defined as "nonforgetfulness." It is the poet, he says, who is the magical, shamanic master of remembering, who calls to mind, for our deepest benefit, the absolute, hidden secrets of our lives. The poet is a detective, and the detective a poet.

The greatest secret, the object of theological detecting, is God, known classically as *deus absconditus,* the hidden one. Even in stories of professional detectives who seek out a solution to a murder or a theft, the mystery runs far deeper than the presenting problem. It is surely too literal to end our detecting by identifying the person who committed the deed. Motive is an important element in most detective stories, but what exactly does motive mean? Who or what drives a person to kill or steal? Why is crime part of existence at all? Who is the God that would create a world riddled with evil?

If we are drawn to watch or read yet another story about a crime and its solving, maybe what draws our attention is the deep crime in which we are all implicated—Adam's transgression, the mythic disobedience, and the loss of Eden. And if we never tire of mystery stories, then maybe we have not yet detected the real mystery.

The detective may be clever like Perry Mason, or unpredictably prescient like Dupin, or preternaturally rational like Sherlock Holmes. The detective is often mercurial—dopey on the surface but crafty underneath, like Columbo or even Inspector Clouseau. Full frontal detecting, the prosaic work of establishment inspectors, is usually exposed for the shallowness of its apparently skillful means. Detective stories amuse us by giving us insight into our own mystery and perhaps shedding light on the ultimate crime, which is the daring transgression involved in being alive at all. We are all children of Adam, the archetypal master criminal. We were all once at home in Eden, which we lost because of a crime we once committed but have now forgotten. We keep trying to detect this mystery and find the criminal, but we keep looking in the wrong place.

We are by September and yet my flowers are bold as June.
Amherst has gone to Eden. To shut our eyes is Travel. The
Seasons understand this. How lonesome to be an Article!
I mean—to have no soul.

Emily Dickinson[9]

THE SMALL WORLD OF OUR DAILY AFFAIRS IS THE COSMOS IN MINIATURE.

Emily Dickinson was one of America's most profound and imaginative artists, and yet she lived most of her life on the fourteen acres of the Dickinson homestead in Amherst, Massachusetts. There she beheld the entire world—nature, culture, human passion, and artistic expressiveness. In her early thirties she summarized her life in a letter to Thomas Wentworth Higginson, who was the first to recognize her creative daimon and genius. She wrote, "You ask of my Companions Hills—Sir—and the Sundown—and a Dog."

The utter transparency and sophisticated innocence in this letter are potent when read in our age of guile and studied opacity. Higginson described his first meeting with Dickinson in a letter of his own: "She came to me with two day lilies which she put in a sort of childlike way into my hand & said 'These are my introduction' in a soft frightened breathless childlike voice."[10] No doubt these daylilies came from her garden, which spread out from the side of her house.

For nine years I practiced psychotherapy one block from Emily Dickinson's grave and lived near the homestead. One summer my wife set up her easel in the Dickinson garden and painted her impressions of a single tree. We toured her house just once, with a talented and sensitive Irishman whom I offended unintentionally. Dickinson was equally sensitive, so much so that today some scholars make a career of studying her neuroses.

Emily Dickinson lived the philosophy of William Blake: To see the world in a grain of sand and eternity in an hour. For her the universe lay spread out before her on fourteen acres of gardens and lawns and in the hills she could make out in the distance, as you can still do today from the upper rooms of the homestead.

Each artist seems to have access to a special chink in the opacity of the cosmos, a crack through which they can perceive the whole and make a philosophy and a life of it. Can't we, too, find our own way to look at our small worlds and perceive the universe—the All manifested by the ordinarily Small? In that way, our lives would take on their proper dimensions, which are measured by time and eternity, place and infinity.

It takes eyes calibrated to the wide world, which can observe the most commonplace event or article and glimpse the incursions of eternity. This capacity gives meaning to ordinary days and liberates us from the unnecessary task of finding meaning outside our own limited lives. All that is required is imagination, a poet's perspective, eyes that see through sensations to their emotional and intellectual core.

One finds meaning in life by living fully and intensely, like the sensitive and self-conscious belle of Amherst, within the borders of one's own particular, vernacular, unexceptional existence.

Monk: "What is Zen?"
Tosu (Zen Master): "Zen."
D. T. Suzuki, *Zen and Japanese Culture*[11]

Lɪᴠɪɴɢ ɪɴ ᴛʜᴇ ᴍᴏᴍᴇɴᴛ ɪs ᴀʟʟ ᴛʜᴇʀᴇ ɪs, ʏᴇᴛ ɪᴛ ɪs ɴᴏᴛ ᴇɴᴏᴜɢʜ.

I was lecturing in one of my favorite venues, the C. G. Jung Educational Center in Houston, Texas, when a woman in the audience said, "I used to look for meaning everywhere, but from now on I'm just going to live with what is." Without thinking I replied, "The trouble is, what is, isn't." There is nothing outside our particular imagination of what is, nothing more pure, and that imagination is more complicated than our intention to deal too purely only with what is.

I felt that she was doing something that I have done many times in my life: finding a subtle, intelligent defense against life's complexity. The Jungian analyst and poet Patricia Berry says that we are only able to defend ourselves against some life necessity when we find a defense that is so airtight and so reasonable that it doesn't look like a defense at all. That is how I felt about the remark about dealing only with what is. If we take literally the statement that only what is counts, then we have bracketed out life as it presents itself, opting for our fantasy of simple, clarified existence.

The idea of dealing only with what is is very different from facing life with all its contrary emotions, personal history, and complicated relationships. The complex mess of life, unfortunate from a certain point of view, is exactly what is. And so are the anxieties and memories and anticipations. They all exist in the precious present and constitute what is.

Maybe what the Zen master is pointing to is the possibility of living concretely rather than abstractly, with originality rather than with a good idea. In that case, the *philosophy* of living in the moment is the worst possible way of life because it is abstract. To find ourselves in the present, we may have to give up any program or idea of living in the present, because being present is not the same as trying to be present. Anyway, what is never will be.

It might be better to surrender cleverness altogether. Correct thinking gets us nowhere. Being smart about life only keeps us from living it. The story beneath the statement that I want to live only in the moment is a tale of wanting to avoid life's complexity, and, paradoxically, by opting for the idea of what is, we successfully avoid the isness that is full in our face.

The impetus for dealing only with what is may be rooted in a spirit imagination of pristine clarity. If only life were simple, separated from the haunting past, the underworld of emotions and desires, and connections with the rest of the world! It may be equally important to deal with what was and what appears to be beneath the surface of things.

As far as I know, the Zen master doesn't advise living in the moment or facing only what is. The Zen poet says:

The wild geese do not intend to cast their reflection
The water has no mind to receive their image.[12]

Things happen without any intention to make them happen. We become involved in situations that we may try to own but that resist ownership. Things happen freely. Giving up the ego satisfaction of feeling in control and at the center of the action is a pure way simply to be. But the *idea* of being in the eternal now, dealing only with what is, is not pure but puristic. In the end, it only distracts us from what could be.

blushes beautifully, embraces
father's neck sweetly:"Father, dearest, please!
let me enjoy virginity forever! Diana's father
let her!"he:"alright"

Ovid[13]

THE SOUL NEEDS REGRESSION AS MUCH AS IT NEEDS EVOLUTION, DEVELOPMENT, AND PROGRESS.

The story of Daphne is one of the classic tales that is never far from my mind. I'm drawn to it like a salmon to its birthplace. Something of my nature is there, and I keep writing and thinking about it.

Daphne is an Artemis woman, a huntress who wants nothing to do with civilization or life with a man. Like all Artemis people, she likes to run. One day Apollo sees her and is wildly attracted to her. He wants to possess her in some way, but she runs from his advances. Her flight inspires him even more. Finally she cries out for help, and her father, a shape-shifting river and an expert metamorphoser, transforms her into a tree. When Apollo catches up with her, he can only wrap his arms about the bark of her trunk.

Something in us doesn't want to be civilized, linked too closely with Apollo and all his humanitarian accomplishments—medicine, music, ideas. It doesn't want any kind of union, but desperately tries to preserve its individuality and integrity. Something in us wants to be wooden, untalkative, and impenetrable. It wants to revert to dumb nature. Something in us doesn't want to be loved or desired. A tree's beauty is purely unintended and purposeless.

Daphne is wooden. She is that which doesn't want to be communicative, available, friendly, present, or articulate. Instinctively she flees from the most noble of attentions, the most humane of admirers. She would rather be like a tree than a person, an it rather than a thou. The Daphne spirit is so pure that it has no use for the sentimentality of relationship.

Modern psychological thinking doesn't appreciate the necessity presented in this myth. We consider it normal and healthy to be intimate with each other and to communicate well. We interpret flight from intimacy as neurotic, abnormal, and practically immoral. But within this myth, flight from interpersonal contact is the norm. Resistance to humanitarian sensitivity is valid. Disappearing from the human scene somehow protects and preserves Daphne in a completely acceptable way.

Rather than judge each other and ourselves for our failure to be sociable, we might reconsider our biases and assumptions, even our sentimentality, about relationship. Perhaps some of our narcissism is a symptomatic attempt to recover a strong unrelated sense of self. How can we reach out to another, anyway, if we don't have strong devotion to our individuality?

Daphne, one of the great mysteries, is the soul in its solitariness. She would rather be with animals than with humans, as any of us might sometimes feel, especially when we have been the victim of human atrocity or stupidity. As a teacher I often thought of the resistance of my students to learning not as a personality problem, but as the necessary unwillingness of the Daphne soul to submit too much to our humanitarian insistence on enculturation.

This is not to say that we should not be close to people, treat them as persons rather than things, and allow ourselves to be led into community and culture. But there is a spirit, Daphne, that also preserves our pristine individuality and protects us from being lost in the unconsciousness of the well-intentioned culture or the loving partner. Children are especially motivated by Daphne; they are led into civilized life kicking and screaming, often preferring the unsocial behavior of their defining myth to the contaminating rules of society.

I will kiss you when
I cut up one dozen new men
and you will die somewhat,
again and again.
Anne Sexton[14]

J EALOUSY IS A NATURAL, CREATIVE HUMAN EMOTION
THAT CAN GET OUT OF HAND.

In the great goddess Hera, the Greeks give us a strange yet beautiful image of
jealousy. She was honored as the icon of marriage and fidelity, yet she was also
known to fall into wild, destructive jealous rages. In spite of their arguments,
which could assume colossal and devastating proportions, Zeus and Hera, the
archetypal married couple, were honored as the very exemplars of intimate
and lasting union.

This old tale suggests that jealousy and the union of hearts go hand in hand.
Of course we don't enjoy the feelings of jealousy, and it is easy to imagine them
to be neurotic. We might believe that jealousy is a personal failure and that we
should be above such a paltry emotion, but at that moment of disclaiming we
may be most ripe for its lessons.

Newspapers remind us how often jealousy turns violent. It is frequently at
the base of domestic abuse and not uncommonly leads to murder. It is a dangerous emotion. In therapy I have often dealt with jealousy at the edge of vio-

lence, and I have seen up close how paranoia and rage blend in a threatening emotional concoction. This is not a mood to take lightly, and yet at the same time it may be foolish to try to rise above it.

Jealousy is fueled by powerful, blinding masochism, in which the offended person revels in his or her victimization. Deep satisfaction rises out of each new offense or suspicion. The masochist searches for evidence that will inflict more pain and takes delight in increasingly abhorrent discoveries. Jealousy demonstrates the joy of suffering and the allure of pain.

On the principle that a symptom points to what is lacking and needed, vehement masochism betrays the fact that the jealous person will not surrender to the dictates of life. The victim desperately tries not to be wounded, doesn't want the other to have a life or any free will, can't stand the thought of the loved one being charmed by any other person. The madly jealous person wants unmitigated control and possession, wants nothing of surrender and no loss of power.

If a friend or therapist suggests lightening up and letting life go its own way, the jealous person will not be persuaded, because this dark passion is not reasonable. It is an expression of the soul, not of the ego. It is in the nature of things, not an opinion or attitude that can easily be changed. You see jealousy in animals, and sometimes you wonder if rainy weather is not jealous of sunshine. Giordano Bruno told a story about mountains in competition with each other.

The solution might be to avoid reasonable resolutions altogether and instead allow the ruinous feelings and thoughts to do their torturous work. Jealousy initiates us all into the deep laws of life. It doesn't merely teach, it etches its particular truths into the heart by drawing emotional blood, an ingredient in all genuine initiations.

According to one story, in jealousy and in the spirit of competition with her husband, Hera gave birth to a badly formed child, Hephaistos, and was so angry that she tossed him through the air down into the sea. This mythic fall of Hephaistos gives us a clue about jealousy. Usually we seek out only good experiences and harmonious emotions, especially in our relationships. But Hera, the complete goddess of marriage and vitality, bore a wounded child who, due to his mother's rage, like Adam and Humpty-Dumpty had a great fall. Crippled by this flare-up of violence, he was nevertheless the master craftsman for the world and for the gods. We, too, may be wounded by our jealousy, but that doesn't mean we are not fit for a creative life.

The story implies that our passion for union with another, completed by its jealousies, competitiveness, and possessiveness, is creative precisely in those areas where its form is not perfect and perhaps not even acceptable. In our jealousy we fall into our deep humanity, just as Adam and Eve fell into human life by dint of their insuppressable appetites.

Jealousy is nothing to be proud of and certainly not something to seek out. But when it occurs, we may know that our passion is strong and our psyche puerile. We need only learn deeper lessons about love and union, and especially how to surrender to the gifts and losses of abundant providence. Life provides, but it also takes away. It is bitterly painful to learn this lesson, and if we resist it too strongly we may act out our ignorance and immaturity violently. All the same, each pang of jealousy offers a way to enter more profoundly into ripened life and open-hearted love.

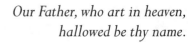
Our Father, who art in heaven,
hallowed be thy name.

PATRIARCHY IS A FORM OF CREATIVITY THAT NEEDS
TO BE REDISCOVERED IN OUR TIME.

Feminists have rightly complained about the devastating effects of a certain kind of patriarchy that has jealously kept women out of places of influence and power and has led to extreme instances of injustice. But the justified assault on patriarchy has been indiscriminate, weakening our appreciation for the importance of fatherhood and masculinity. In spite of the oppressions of a male-dominant society, we need strong, wise, paternal guidance and protection, whether that spirit appears in institutions, in ways men live their lives, or even in women.

We should be able to distinguish between the paternal spirit, with all its benefits, and paternalism, which is a manipulative, self-serving exploitation of fatherhood. Every once in a while a political leader appears who is full of wisdom and personal strength. His words are trustworthy and worth listening to, and his leadership transcends self-aggrandizement. In him we sense a deep-seated, porous, and selfless father spirit. Too often, of course, leaders speak the language of authentic paternal wisdom but their actions show that they don't understand the meaning of their own words. Others courageously dare to embody the father spirit without using it for their personal advantage. Gandhi did not show a need to grasp power for himself, and he offered challenging guidance along the path of nonviolence. Martin Luther King led with a style and philosophy light years distant from the usual, acting effectively and powerfully without conjuring up oppressive paternalism.

The father spirit that seeds culture and personality is a subtle substance. We may recognize strands of traditional paternal qualities in it—guidance, protection, procreativity, teaching, and genuine leadership. This spirit is so subtle that although we see it clearly in a confident man, we might also glimpse it in a woman of vision, a pioneering community, or even a forceful but imperturbable building.

We have weakened the nobility of fatherhood in our time by mistaking imperialism in business and government for genuine paternal leadership. Mistakenly we complain about patriarchy instead of paternalism and weak-kneed authority. *Patri-archy* refers to the archetypal or original father, the ur-father, the father in heaven who permeates every created thing with his seminal possibilities.

It is no wonder that fathers today are confused about how to be and therefore surrender their role. Our criticisms have obscured the archetype, and in all areas of life we are left without the leadership and procreativity we need. Procreativity differs from plain creativity in that specifically it seeds a future, offering confidence and hope. It sustains and teaches the new generation instead of being afraid of it. Mythology warns us of the tendency to fear the future generation as an emasculating threat, and current politics demonstrates that fear. In America today, many leaders honor 1940s patriotism and fear 1960s vitality.

We might deal better with virulent paternalism by giving new honor to fatherhood and strong, wise leadership than by creating a climate of criticism around all attempts at being a father. We might take on the challenge of fatherhood with new vision rather than skirt it. We might reimagine our educational institutions around the theme of father and his stand-in, Mentor, rather than more abstractly as the genderless, mechanical dissemination of information. Rather than disseminate, we might simply seminate—seed and create life.

The father becomes a problem only when his deep and subtle spirit disappears and is replaced not by a mentor but by an impostor. Paternalism, like any ism, is a disguised and corrupt version of the real thing. Yes, he needs to go, but we must take care lest when we banish the imperial impostor, we lose the Father Almighty.

I am the woman of an ancient master
to whom I swore eternal devotion
I am a woman of colored glass
through whom passes every changing with colors
I am the woman of No One
and perhaps I am not even a woman.

Matilde Jonas[15]

Gender is infinitely more subtle than biological difference and is never static.

Generally our thinking moves directly from anatomical difference to psychological differentiation and we assume that there are two genders, just as there are two biological sexes. But a human being is never reducible to biology. To make that reduction is to enter the fallacy of physicalism—the idea that a human being can be defined and then treated as a material body. This fallacy overlooks a world of emotion, memory, fantasy, and meaning, all of which more directly define a human being than the body pictured on a doctor's skeleton chart of bone and organs.

Gender is a state of mind, a product of the imagination. One man experiences masculinity in a way entirely different from another. The femininity of a particular woman is unique, an aspect of her personality or, even deeper, a manifestation of her soul. The many images of woman we find in mythology, from the battle-ready Athena to the adorned and perfumed Aphrodite to the woodswoman Artemis, are not mere accidental qualities of womanhood; they are radically unique ways in which femininity shows itself and is experienced. The same applies to the male figures of myth and fiction, each of which shows how gender is woven into the thick fabric of personality.

Gender is archetypal, and I can think of no better way to deepen the liberation of women and the feminine spirit, both of which could save our society from self-destructive violence, than to pore over great mythological, religious, and literary images of men and women, discovering what it means to be human and how our humanity finds shimmering nuance through the sheer radiance of our gender.

In my adolescence I lived in a religious order dedicated to the Virgin Mary in her sorrow. Mater Dolorosa was the name of my high school. In the purple atmosphere of this image I became intimate with the feminine coloring of depression. The sad mother lives profoundly and actively in me. She is behind my thoughts about depression and is my tutor in psychology. She is a melancholy, sophisticated aspect of the Artemis woman—the feminine spirit of integrity, solitude, and chastity. Unlike the modern person who rushes to drug his depression, she owns up to her sadness and allows it to penetrate her thoroughly and then define her.

We could explore the stories of the Virgin Mary, Artemis, Venus, Psyche, Penelope, Hera, Judith, Lilith, Madame Bovary, Candy, Virginia Woolf, Margaret Fuller, and many, many others to deepen our sense of what a woman is and what femininity means, without ever arriving at a conclusion, but all the way being inspired to honor and treasure the image that emerges. We might learn how precious this feminine spirit is, how wonderful to have it in our lives.

Gender is an aspect of our individuality. I am a man as no one else is a man. My masculinity is like my American spirit, a defining facet. The variations of gender are infinite, and so it is absurd to reduce gender to two categories and insist that everyone fit into one or the other. Besides, all dualisms doom us to division and conflict. They are simplistic descriptions of experience and tend toward easy literalism. Paradoxically, to become less certain about one's own gender may be the turning point at which one begins to discover the richness of one's masculinity and femininity.

Each Daimon is drawn to whatever man or,
if its nature is more general,
to whatever nation it most differs from,
and it shapes into its own image the
antithetical dream of man or nation.

W. B. Yeats[16]

Nᴏᴛ ᴄᴏɴꜱᴄɪᴏᴜꜱɴᴇꜱꜱ ᴀɴᴅ ꜱᴇʟꜰ-ᴜɴᴅᴇʀꜱᴛᴀɴᴅɪɴɢ ʙᴜᴛ ᴀ ᴘᴀꜱꜱɪᴏɴᴀᴛᴇ ɪɴɴᴇʀ ᴘʀᴇꜱᴇɴᴄᴇ ᴍᴀᴋᴇꜱ ᴜꜱ ᴡʜᴀᴛ ᴀɴᴅ ᴡʜᴏ ᴡᴇ ᴀʀᴇ.

In rationalistic times like ours it is tempting to think that we are shaped by our intentions and our awareness. We think that the ego is the dominant self, and we educate ourselves to have good ego boundaries, strong identity, and self-esteem. But more enchanted philosophies recognize that we are made from the depths, from beyond consciousness. We are more original than we can imagine. We are driven from a place beneath awareness, and what drives us—it has been called angel, daimon, animus, duende—hurls us toward our identity and our place in time and space.

W. B. Yeats saw that the daimon, the inner presence that is full of power and the ultimate source of our real creativity, is an antithetical self, an opposite, a spirit that is brought to a host precisely and utterly different from itself, so that we often feel both conflict and resource in relation to the spirit that makes us passionate. It may take us in directions that inspire fear. It may demand a response that we don't particularly enjoy and that seems to contradict our nature.

In my own case, I can't understand how someone like me, who is uncomfortable in social situations and who loves solitude and privacy, seems to have been called to a relatively public life. I have many friends who seek out a life of public recognition, the opportunity to speak and teach and occasions to travel, and are not given the opportunities. I don't care for any of these experiences, and yet they seem to be part of my calling. To that extent, I am always working against myself, and yet I find creative work flowing from this contradiction. I'm also certain that it is my deepest nature to be unmarried, alone, and quiet, and yet at the same time I feel most alive and graced by my marriage and my children.

We may each have an idea of who we should be, knowing the seeds of a self for many years. But our idea of who we are and the direction we ought to go may be entirely thwarted by circumstances and fate. We may discover that we are most ourselves when we are furthest from the self we think we ought to be.

It should now be possible to shift from the modern self that is defined as an ego to a more archaic notion, where the self is deeper than consciousness and rises sometimes like a beast from a mysterious land beneath ordinary life, an Atlantis of the soul. To be open to these inspirations and to allow these other antithetical selves to express their yearnings is to discover an intensity of life otherwise not available.

Writing about duende, the inspiring and enlivening spirit throbbing within any vital activity, Federico García Lorca says that it rises up from the feet, that we "climb each step in the tower of our perfection" by fighting the duende, and that there are no maps or disciplines to help us find it. We will not have a strong sense of self until and unless we sense the wind of this spirit in our words and actions, and yet no one can teach us how to reach this point.

Toss out all the subtle egotism of modern psychology, and perhaps in that gap, in that place of discomforting contradiction, there may appear the distant sound of an antithetical voice that is at once threatening and saving. Our life is then a response, our creativity a surrender.

The soul is filled throughout with discord and dissonance,
and so its first need is poetic madness. That way through
musical sounds we can waken what is dormant, through sweet
harmonies calm what is turbulent, and through the blending
of various elements quell the discord and temper the different
parts of the soul.

Marsilio Ficino[17]

The soul is not nearly as rational as the ego.

It is essential in modern life to adore the ego, to think that our social problems and our personal struggles will be resolved once we understand the situation and gain control of it. The current idea of a well-adjusted person is one who is unusually conscious and in charge. It is assumed that the purpose of life is to be more of an ego, successful in the eyes of the world and sanctioned by a swelling egotistic bank account.

The self-reliance characteristic of those who live by the philosophy of modernism betrays its secular core. Other communities of the past and present who live by traditional values acknowledge the mystery of human existence and the immensity of nature. Faced with obstacles, they pray, sacrifice, praise, and petition the source of life beyond themselves. Their religion is not just belief, but a way of being in the world and a profound conception of the self.

One way tends toward hubris and self-interest, while the other is rooted in humility.

When we live from a deeper place, we become palpably aware that life is fundamentally mysterious and is ultimately incomprehensible to our rational ways of thinking. We realize that we need other kinds of intelligence and skills. Traditional societies could instruct us in these areas. They worship their ancestors, while we blame our insecurities on our parents and grandparents. They instruct their children in the myths and rites that hold both society and the self together, while we teach our children how to count and use a computer. They heal body, soul, and spirit in one, while we break ourselves into compartments and rely on experts trained in isolated specialties.

As we move closer to a soulful life, we learn to live with unruly passions and unpredictable fantasies. We live with our madness and move with it gracefully. Psychosis is not real madness, but is an excess of ego that fractures the envelope in which soul and self lie encircled in each other. Neurosis is the failure to weave autonomous fantasy and stirring emotion into life and is the visible sign of a divided self. The ideal is not to become sane and hygienic, but to live creatively by responding positively to the powerful moods, feelings, and ideas that captivate us. If we don't meet these life-shaping expressions of the soul creatively, they will quickly become adversaries, and we will develop the split psyche so characteristic of our times, in which our sane lives are flat and aimless while our passions seem incomprehensible and out of control.

To deal with the powerful urges of the deep soul, a poetic attitude rather than a rational one is more effective. Wisdom rather than information guides us, providing the patience to become acquainted with the soul rather than the impatience that leads us into quick cures and explanations. The point is not to flee our depths but to reconnect with them.

The arts could serve us well in this process if we made connections between our experiences of drama, literature, painting, and music and our most personal conflicts and challenges. The arts meet us at the point of imagination, which is a blending of reason and mystery in images. In the arts we contemplate our world and have the chance no longer to be strangers to the deep self that is as opaque to reason as it is transparent to the imagination. An art image is psychosis contained, undivided, and constructive.

In a time of emotional struggle, it might be better to listen to a special piece of music than to consult an expert, and better to draw a picture of the situation than to try to figure it out. Reason is distant and has its own limited requirements for an ordered life, while the arts are intimate and can hold almost any conceivable human predicament.

For look, how oft I iterate the work,
So many times, I add unto his virtue.

Ben Jonson, *The Alchemist*, II.iii.106–107

Lᴵꜰᴇ ᴍᴏᴠᴇꜱ ɪɴ ᴄɪʀᴄʟᴇꜱ, ᴄʏᴄʟᴇꜱ, ᴀɴᴅ ᴄɪʀᴄᴜᴍᴀᴍʙᴜʟᴀᴛɪᴏɴꜱ.

Humans often have a preference for straight lines. We think of evolution and human development as following an uncrooked path toward perfection. We expect our neighbors to walk the straight and narrow. We don't approve of deviancy (*de via*), which is nothing more than veering off the straight line. Furthermore, we understand that the best straight line of evolution and development moves forward. We don't think much of regression.

It's interesting, then, that alchemists of old, who saw their work with metals and chemicals as a reflection of the soul's processes, described the task as one of cycling and circling. The opus, the work of alchemy, was called *rotatio* or *circulatio*. The vessel in which the work took place, shaped like a bird with its neck bent over plucking its breast, was sometimes described as a pelican. This shape allowed the material to circulate endlessly.

I see my own life as a recycled version of my family's quirks, strengths, and weaknesses. I look at my hands sometimes and see my father's. I feel a strong reserve in my approach to people, and I sense my mother's sensitivity. I feel my grandfather's humor in me and my uncle's unlimited tolerance. I do the family blush about sex, and I have its homebound view of the world.

In therapy, several men and women who had been married more than once or had had many lovers told me of their resolution to finally straighten out and move on. They were tired of the cycles in which they repeated destructive choices. But I didn't have much faith in their resolutions. It might have been better, I thought, if they reflected positively on the repetitions that fueled their desires rather than hoped for a release from the bondage of their nature.

One sometimes sentimental way of redeeming the soul's circlings is to insist that they are, after all, spirals. We are getting someplace even if we're going in circles. But I don't trust this clever spin on circles either. A circle is a circle, and there is no reason to believe that human life is correct only when it straightens out. Maybe at root we are coils of possibility in constant rotation.

Rainer Maria Rilke said, "I live my life in widening rings." It may well be useful to note the expanding of the circles in which we live, but it is also important not to lose the sensation of cycles, which may be painful to anyone living in a culture dedicated to the extending line. Maybe in life we never really develop, but only expand the rotations that give us our firm identity. Maybe we should expect always to get into familiar trouble and to repeat both the glorious and the defeating themes that are embedded in our soul.

Traditional peoples apparently honor the cycles of nature, communities, and persons with as much fervor as we honor developments and growth. I sense escape in theories of expansion, because it may be that the soul finds its way by not going anywhere. The circling of nature, inner and outer, may be the best way to find our substance.

We might know ourselves better and be closer to our nature by honoring these cycles rather than by running away from them in sentimental philosophies of growth. I don't grow, I am. I don't change, I merely manifest differently the prime material with which I am born. Perhaps if we got off the demanding belt of change and growth, we might relax into the circumambulations of life that turn us over and over, polishing the arcane stone of our most essential selves, revealing more and more of who and what we are.

Modern psychology tries to tell us that we are constantly developing creatures, but I prefer to think of us as seasonal beings. We have our summers of sunny pleasure and our winters of discontent, our springtimes of renewal and our autumns of necessary decay. We are essentially rhythmic, musical. As the ancients used to say, our emotions are in orbit, like the planets. Patterns that define us return again and again, and in these returns we find our substance and our continuity, our original nature and our identity.

Under every deep a lower deep opens.
Ralph Waldo Emerson[18]

BENEATH THE FAVORITE TALE OF THE MOMENT A DEEPER STORY ALWAYS LIES WAITING TO BE DISCOVERED.

When I was practicing therapy, one of my "techniques" was first to listen to the story a client told me and then to find ways to deepen that story. This approach required restraint on my part because it is always tempting, when we hear a piece of someone else's fiction about life, to counter it with our own. This loyalty to one's own myth is understandable because our story is the most precious thing we have. Our lives depend on it. Still, one of the beautiful aspects of social living is the opportunity to meet others who live by a different fiction.

For instance, a woman might come into therapy complaining that in her adult life she could never enjoy a good relationship with a man because in her childhood her father had been emotionally cool and distant in relation to her. The story is very convincing, and at a certain level it is no doubt true. She believes in it with all her heart. But her story, for all its validity and usefulness, may have negative consequences.

She may, for example, feel alienated from her father because the story carries a degree of blame. The story shifts the weight of her failures in love to her father. Having shifted the responsibility, she feels lighter, but her story places her in a mirror version of the father story. Now she is cool and distant in relation to him.

The story is also far from complete, although it may appear to be a final explanation. Whenever a story puts an end to reflection and further storytelling, that story is now serving as a defense. The whole point of a good story is to give birth to other stories and to deeper reflection. As I sat in therapy, hour after hour, I took notice of the quality of the stories being told. I tried not to take them literally as presented because then I would be nothing more than a cohort in a strategy of defense. The poetics in a person's story is its opening toward insight, its invitation to go further in reflection. Therapy may be defined as a deepening of the story being lived and told.

To deepen the story, I might explore certain themes and narratives. "What did your father do when he acted remote and cool? How did other people react to his frigidity? Where do you think he got this attitude or habit? Was your mother different in this respect? Do the families of your mother and father differ in their emotional tone? What about your father's parents—were they like him? How did he feel about having a daughter?"

With all these questions, I'm not seeking a final explanation, but rather expanding the stories into subplots and minor characters. I have no intention of tracking down a culprit. I only want a fuller story. As a starting point for dialogue, I would like to know the imaginal landscape in which my client has built her emotional homestead.

Another approach might be to look for other sources of narratives at work in the woman's life. Usually we found rich motifs in dreams, which led the life narrative in more subtle directions. The woman might dream that she was being driven in a car by an unknown man or by her current lover. This might lead us to imagine her situation as one of control. Maybe she falls into the cultural habit of granting the man too much power. I often heard dreams from women in particular of stairways and elevators, indicating that the issue was a vertical one. I remember one woman's dream in which she was halfway along on the up escalator when she saw her loved one passing her on the down escalator. Everyone tells us to go up into awareness and perfection, but the life we're looking for may be lower, beneath our present understanding rather than above it.

The story within and beneath the familiar story is almost always full of insight and new possibility. It may take courage to go another level down, to abandon clarity, however illusory, for confusion and puzzlement. Our habitual stories usually protect us from the mystery of our lives. But there is always the opportunity to take our storytelling deeper, always the chance to find the intelligence and comfort we have been seeking at a level far beneath the basement of our expectations.

THE PROJECT OF BEING A SELF IS THE SUREST WAY
NEVER TO FEEL LIKE A PERSON.

An old Jewish joke: A rabbi raises his hands wildly in prayer. "I'm nobody," he proclaims fervently. A student sees the prayer and prostrates himself, raises his arms, and cries wildly, "I'm nobody." A janitor in the temple sees them both, falls on his knees, flails his arms, and shouts, "I'm nobody." The rabbi watches and says to the student, "Who does he think he is?"

People today are so uncertain about having an identity that they make a project out of it. They want to grow and self-actualize. They want to become a somebody, and they honor, all out of proportion, those who have become supersomebodies—celebrities.

The secret is that each of us is a somebody from birth. We come with original somebodyhood because we each have a soul. At the beginning, we are not, as modern thought would have us believe, a tabula rasa, an empty slate. We are persons who are offered the experience of our individuality for a lifetime, no matter how long that lasts. But today we have forgotten about the soul, which is the source of personality. We see ourselves as milk bottles at birth, empty and spanking clean, waiting to be filled up.

It is the soul that offers us a sense of identity, and it is the daimon, the other self, in Yeats's words, that brings us into full possession of our capacity as a self. Lacking an appreciation for the deep soul that bears our sense of self, we seek it in the wrong places and imagine it in the wrong way. This self is not something to be fabricated by achievement, cleverness, training, or learning. It is not the product of self-analysis or understanding. It is a gift, waiting to be accepted and nurtured in its unfolding.

We don't have to merit being an individual, but we can lose that awareness through a skewed focus on life. Then we feel insecure and make too much of an effort to retrieve what we assume we never had in the first place. Somebodies are out of touch with the nobody that would liberate them from the self project. Being quintessentially ordinary helps us find the liminal place where somebodyness and nobodyness come together, where the burden of having to have a personality is eased. Narcissism is a profound uncertainty as to whether you can get along not being somebody, but living in full cognizance of the soul grants solid identity no matter what is happening on the surface.

Late in life I became a sort of somebody. In the limited circles of those who read serious books on spirit and soul, I was a personality. But I found many leaking holes in this recognition. Once I was being interviewed on a radio program I liked, and the very gifted and talented host told me he hadn't had time to read my book because he'd had to prepare for another guest who had more somebodyness that I had. Once I sat signing books at an author's table in a California bookstore when, in the midst of my fifteen minutes of being an author signing books, the manager tore down my picture and display to get ready for the next celebrity. I discovered the cruelty of the pecking order that wouldn't exist for someone who wasn't a somebody.

Being a somebody is also difficult for some people around me, who become nobodies in the glare of attention to another. I have also been on the receiving end of that neglect. I was once having dinner with the actor André Gregory in a restaurant in Greenwich Village that he frequented. The owner came to our table several times to make sure everything was all right, and each time, he spoke to André without ever letting his eyes turn in my direction. In the glow of the somebodyhood of my actor friend, I didn't exist.

Being someone special also sets you up for attacks by those very people who acknowledge your individuality but also resent it or envy it. Because you are somebody, they are jealous and hold you accountable for sundry violations. A person of prominence is handy for displacing blame.

Many want to be somebodies, and that appetite is probably natural and fine, but it can also be a distraction from the rich life available midway between being somebody and nobody. We may think we'd like to taste the life of celebrity, but those who have it, although they enjoy its perks, also feel its drawbacks and dangers—the obvious ones like lack of privacy and public criticism, and the less obvious such as disappointment that being a celebrity doesn't solve the riddle of life. One may be surprised to learn that the hunger to feel one's substance remains until it finally fades in the radiance of nobodyness.

Maybe it isn't literal celebrity we long for, but the sense that life has meaning, that we belong on this earth, that we are contributing, and that we are appreciated. Being a celebrity doesn't guarantee these necessities, and indeed it may profoundly disappoint our expectations. But the thing for which being a celebrity is only a symptom is the strong sense of self offered by one's passion, one's real substance, and true and heartfelt recognition from the people around us.

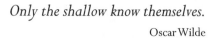

Sᴇʟꜰ-ᴜɴᴅᴇʀꜱᴛᴀɴᴅɪɴɢ ɪꜱ ɴᴏᴛ ᴀꜱ ɪᴍᴘᴏʀᴛᴀɴᴛ ᴀꜱ ʟɪᴠɪɴɢ ꜰʀᴏᴍ ᴛʜᴇ ꜱᴏᴜʟ.

During my years of doing therapy, it was not unusual for a client to say, "If only I could finally understand myself and figure out what I'm doing, I'd be a free person." One of the great unconscious beliefs of our time is our trust in the mind. We try to understand every fragment of the natural world, celebrating discoverers, inventors, researchers, and analysts, and we apply that same passion to ourselves. We want to discover, interpret, analyze, and reinvent ourselves over and over.

What struck me in therapy was the hollowness in most self-understanding. A man or woman would tell me one day that they finally understood what was going on in their lives, then the next week they would present an entirely new idea about themselves. Sometimes this chain of self-understanding would get

72

quite long, and most surprising of all, these achievements in understanding had no effect on the clients' quality of life. They canvassed the list of experienced personalities but never seemed to touch the original self.

What then, you might ask, was the purpose of therapy: to continue to analyze the process?

There were many things going on. For example, without necessarily understanding it, we connected with the past, expanding the sense of self to include persons involved in our origins. Usually we think of the self as an ego contained in the skin of personality, but a deeper self, a more original self, lies outside the time and space of our personal lives. What was your face before you were born? the Zen master asks. It is an excellent question, first because it has no definite answer, and second because it breaks through the idea that our personal life begins the day we are conceived or born.

In therapy, we never understood dreams completely, but we developed a closer relationship to the intimate inner world of the imagination. We came to know the myths that were playing in the theater of a life, and that was no small achievement. We glimpsed some of the narrative themes that were influencing life. More importantly, we translated daily experience into the language of dream to glimpse the strong imagination that was at work making meaning.

I saw what we were doing as Dionysian theater—breaking the literal self into pieces in order to see the many dramas that make up a life. The word *analysis* means "to loosen up," and I did what I could to shake free some of the fragments of art and narrative that constitute a personality. Usually life itself was sufficiently volatile, and the dramas and *dramatis personae* were making their appearances without any encouragement.

Some ways of knowing do not require understanding. You don't need to understand a play or a movie to enjoy it. You may know your spouse very well, but as the years go by you understand this person less and less. Yet you are pro-foundly involved in the drama of the marriage. You may know your dog, but you may understand nothing of his experience or nature. You may understand less and less about the world, and yet you might feel more a part of it than ever.

Being familiar with yourself is a form of knowledge, and it, too, doesn't require understanding. You may get to know the images that crowd your dreams and see how they change from one period to the next, but all the while you may not have a clue as to what they mean. I took it to be a rule: The more involved you are, the less you know.

We may come to know our friends and lovers over years of conversation and experience, but we may eventually realize that it is enough to love them without knowing what they are all about. We may not approve of everything they do, and we may not appreciate their eccentric ways, but still we know and appreciate them. We have faith that in the dimness of our ignorance we have the opportunity to give ourselves more fully to their reality. Unconditional love means that we don't love on the condition that we understand.

(Speaking to the soul:) "You taste like a grape."
Mechthild of Magdeburg[19]

W E CAN GRASP THE SOUL MORE DIRECTLY THROUGH THE SENSES THAN BY MEANS OF THE MIND.

Mystics like Mechthild of Magdeburg and Hildegard of Bingen often use poetry to describe the soul and its relation to God, and that poetry is often sensuous in its imagery and allusions. The soul is indeed like a grape, just as a grape is like the soul. Each has an envelope, a skin that holds it together and gives it form, while inside is a mouth-watering, tingling, sweet softness. Certainly the soul sometimes has a deep purple exterior, but even within that bitter skin lies a sweet meat.

We might see every particular of life as an envelope of the soul, and each thing and event has its interior. For over a century psychoanalysis has been charting that interior, but analysis is only one way to perceive it. Another is the way of sensation.

We may think that sensation is a purely physical experience, but it is also a way of imagining. We taste a grape, and we know it firsthand. We know its properties through taste, and then we can go on to find grape poetry everywhere, as did the Greeks and the Christians who followed them. The grape became the image through which to find the God of ecstasy, Dionysus, and the God of Love, Jesus.

The grape, like the soul, has many levels. It can be eaten whole and is often used as a symbol of sensuousness—grapes dropped indulgently into an open mouth. Its juice is nectar, but when it is allowed to ferment, it becomes the source of deeper pleasure and intoxication. The grape, like the soul, has a whole culture around it, as well as art and religious imagery inspired by it. Jesus says, "I am the vine," and wine becomes the centerpiece of his eucharist. Elsewhere, as in the Jewish Purim and Greek libations, it calls forth the religious spirit.

The shadow of the grape is its being crushed to make wine, the insides forced into view and squeezed dry. The soul, of course, also knows what it is to be squeezed painfully. "I'm crushed," we say when the world has fallen in. But even then there is redemption in the collapse of the envelope, when in identification with Dionysus our very souls take on bite, flavor, and potency.

We can find the soul in sensations of taste and intoxication as well as in the kind of crushing that resurrects in character. When we eat a juicy grape or take a sip of wine, we are, as the Catholic Mass exemplifies, taking in a god. The sweet taste and the tangy feel of juice from the grape and the tingle and nose of the wine tell us what we need to know about a certain quality of existence, a divine layer of meaning made accessible through sensations.

This is real mysticism: not a flight from ordinary existence, not a purely intellectual attempt at transcendence, but the discovery of the awful interior of the world and the self within the simple sphere of the grape, the world in miniature, the microcosm explored appropriately and effectively with the tongue.

Here I've no continuing city.
Shaker hymn

THE ULTIMATE CREATIVITY IS TO LIVE MORTALITY
INSTEAD OF AVOIDING IT.

A long life is a blessing, but even the longest lives are brief. As anyone who has entered a midlife crisis knows, as you get older, time moves at a faster tempo and the measure of time grows tight. Do you notice the age of those listed in obituaries, wondering for a moment about the passing of time and your own fate? Do you ever wonder about the meaning of a very brief life? Do you imagine what you will die from, and then maybe even try to avoid that particular kind of death? These stinging reminders of our mortality can wake us up to new life.

One way to live our mortality is to "eat, drink, and be merry." It's not a bad philosophy, especially when it is a piece of a larger picture, but there is another side to becoming acquainted with death. I went through a period in my life when morbid fantasies began to invade my awareness, especially at night before falling asleep. I thought I wouldn't live much longer, and I imagined a serious illness and my parting with my family. I began to fear travel and became overly solicitous about the safety of the children. I worried at the slightest sign of bad health in my wife.

One day a psychic came to our home and read my cards. She asked for a question, and I expressed my concern about my own and everyone else's health. She saw the panic quivering just beneath the calm of my question and asked me, with considerable unaffectedness, why I had such little trust in life. From that moment I began to wrestle with my visitations of morbidity. I gave them a name and recognized them when they appeared. I connected with them and let them do their work on me, although I had no idea what the effect might be. At the same time I didn't encourage them.

Sometimes it seems easier not to live than to give yourself to life. Fantasies of death can be a way of excusing yourself from living, or they may be an escape from the weight and challenge of your destiny. Of course, it's important not to deny death, but it's also important to live every day and every moment with generous courage.

Long life is indeed a blessing, but maybe we overdo our concern for the length of our lives and give insufficient attention to the passion we bring to whatever time we have. The meaning and purpose of life are great mysteries, and in that light a very brief life, of only minutes, can be full and rounded. The soul has appeared in the flesh; then it returns to its home of origin. A life has been lived. I often think of extraordinary individuals who died young: Pico della Mirandola at thirty-one, Shubert at thirty-one, Mozart at thirty-five, D. H. Lawrence at forty-four.

Maybe we don't achieve something grand and heroic in the days of our lives.

Fame and achievement may not be our destiny. It may be sufficient to be here, to open our hearts, take in what is offered, make our contribution at whatever level is granted, and gracefully depart. In any case, I am not the one who should be worried about the planning, for each life seems to have come equipped with its own tempo and timetable.

To live a full life may entail a daily kind of mortality, a continuing death in life. I feel this common presence of death in mortifications that come unbidden with more than sufficient regularity. A project fails, I let down a friend, I forget important considerations, I say the wrong thing, my work isn't up to par, I don't give the children the patience and attention they need, I disappear in a cloud of neurotic tension.

We go on living when meaning fails and when we don't get it right. We go on in the presence of mortification, a word that means simply "death-making," and we become who we are destined to be as much through the death-making as the life-making. Success and happiness are impossible without the continuing nudge of death. Living through our mortifications is the coupon for vitality and the ticket home.

Angel of fire and genitals, do you know slime,
that green mama who first forced me to sing . . . ?
Anne Sexton[20]

OUR SPIRITUAL FIRE NEEDS A BASE IN THE MUDDY EARTH.

The word *Adam* names a being made from earth. In some creation stories, God like a sculptor makes people out of clay. Demeter is a mighty Greek Goddess, yet as goddess of fields and natural growth, she may be caught sight of in a simple shuck of corn or a bead of wheat. Not only do we have bodies full of slimy organs, and urinate and defecate, our minds and imaginations are also of the earth.

I once read that a renowned spiritual teacher, responding to a question about the difficulty of remaining celibate, said that all you have to do is think about what sex is and it's easy to resist. I was disappointed to read that statement coming from a person whom one would expect to be earthy and grounded. Sex is slimy from a certain point of view, but only a spirit delighting in disembodiment would not appreciate the mushy, wet, sensuous body we are and the muddy, naturally decaying world we inhabit.

What would it be like, I wonder, if we were born in some dramatic spiritual way. Say the soul like a sheet of silky gauze fell down from the heavens in a soft flutter? Would that be preferable to the birth of a human being at the fork in the legs amid blood, excrement, and waters? I don't think so, because we are given life by the green mama as well as the angel of fire, and the green mama doesn't think much about what she does. She loves and gives birth and then takes back to herself everything she has birthed.

This mystery of green life can be trusted because it is not self-conscious. By some magical transformative power, the green of the mother's trees and plants overwhelms us with its beauty. I have never forgotten the vision I once had in Ireland of a planted field in spring where the green seemed to burn like fire and glow its truth that nature is godly and full of spirit.

The bodiless spirituality that many find comforting I don't trust. I don't trust its preference for white light and its assumption that the spirit resides in the sky or in the brilliant stars. Even the worship of the sun makes sense only when we include the heliotrope that turns to it and makes green chlorophyll.

When I pray to the green mama I don't worry about her authority or potential for punishment, though I don't want to be misled by her beauty into thinking she isn't deathly and threatening. But she has a mother's way, and that makes all the difference. As Hildegard said so many times, holiness is green, and as Julian of Norwich reminds us, God is a mother.

D. H. Lawrence frequently spoke strongly for a sensual way of life, which he distinguishes from thinking about and merely esteeming sensuality. He was also, in his paganism, one of the most religious of modern poets. We seem not to have learned this lesson that the slimy body close at hand is holier than the dry, distant mind, because we still pray to abstract gods and look beyond the sensuousness of the moment for redemption. Perhaps we don't grasp the mystery found in many religious teachings according to which the spiritual life begins when God becomes incarnate—a fancy word for green slime.

THE SPIRITUAL LIFE IS EQUIVALENT TO LIVING THE POETRY
OF THE WORLD, NOT FACTS.

There are those who believe that the Dogon people of Mali in Africa were once taught by visitors from another planet about the stars, and especially about Sirius and its companion star. The mythologies of these people are used to support the idea that we have been visited by aliens, and the proof is in the simple drawings of an African community. Carl Sagan and others have questioned this assumption, but I want to go beyond disputing the facts to arguing against the approach.

Poetry in the larger sense of the word—poems, stories, myths, paintings, dances, dreams—is the most exhilarating and transporting vehicle for travel there is. More effective than space shuttles, more penetrating than warp-speed starships, and more probing than Mars-rovers, poetry takes us far, far away to a reality that is at once our own and absolutely alien. This would be a trite observation unless perhaps we recalled many ancient teachings that tell of the soul's journeys.

In many areas of life we literalize our wishes. Looking for the sweet life, we eat too much sugar. Wanting to work out the meaning of our lives, we labor too long and too hard. Wanting to live in the land of bodiless spirit, we try to lose weight. And needing to move beyond the facts of a concrete life, we build rocket ships.

In our home we have a telescope that points all day and all night into the sky. When on occasion I look closely at the moon or at the rings of Saturn, I am transported into wonder and wrapped in mystery. And that is enough. I don't need to go to Saturn and get its dust on my feet. I need only wonder about its halos and become mystified by the beauty and the distances and the brightness of the world I inhabit.

I would like to have a chat with a traveler from another planet, but if I did I would do what Carl Sagan and others did. I would play him some Bach and Bob Dylan and show him a Botticelli and watch him turn green with envy—a little green man. But I don't need such a chat because the poetry of the world takes me away. My guess is that the Dogon are among the best poets in the land, and I'd rather contemplate their simple drawings than investigate their possible connivance with lost tourists from Sirius's moon.

I don't much like science fiction, because the emphasis is on science rather than fiction, though I enjoyed the old Star Trek Enterprise because its self-parody was so close and plain. I didn't have to worry about meeting Dr. Spock in my backyard. Anyway, it's obvious that the stories of that voyage are about us, not about them. As long as we confuse these categories, we won't be worthy of a conversation with our brothers from Sirius. I imagine that they will stay away until we can talk to them about the voyages of the poet and truly become transported into another land in another time, until we can meet them and compare notes as soul travelers.

*Is it oblivion or absorption when things
pass from our minds?*
Emily Dickinson[22]

C ONSCIOUSNESS IS A SIGN THAT WE HAVEN'T YET
LEARNED TO LIVE FROM THE SOUL.

I spent many years trying to become conscious, but all that effort led merely
to self-consciousness, which in turn generated guilt, anxiety, and ambition. I
was told that higher consciousness was a worthy goal and that its opposite,
unconsciousness, was the result of laziness and ignorance. Around the age of
fifty, my ideals and values began to change, so much so that many of them
turned upside down and inside out. Now I see great value in laziness, understood as giving up both effort and the attempt to justify my life. I have come to
appreciate the teaching I have found in many religions that praises holy ignorance. And I have been discovering how to live with little consciousness.

Emerson once remarked that it is advisable to live without consciousness of
the workings of the body, and I wonder if the same recommendation applies to
the whole of life. Perhaps in some ways we do have to become conscious, and
that may be the proper work of the first half of life. But then all our education
and learning experiences may fade, not into oblivion, where they are simply

lost, but by a process of absorption into us, so that they become us or we become them.

I have always thought that the most remarkable statement James Hillman ever made about the soul, and he has made many startling observations, is that the soul leads us into unconsciousness, and that for our own benefit. When we fall in love or become absorbed in work or are seized by a powerful depression, we lose control and perspective. The soul takes over and from a dimmer place takes the lead. We don't know exactly what we are doing or whether we should be doing it. By remaining in this psychic fog, we may end up in a place we have been searching for all our lives—with the right person, in a good job, with a new level of self-possession.

Our culture prizes cleverness and self-awareness, but it should be obvious that this approach merely leads to competition and aggression spurred on by anxiety. To live from the mind is to balance in uncertainty on a high wire. The soul is more grounded, and indeed its proper territory seems to be somewhere beneath the ground. There is a fine word for this particular soul and its spirituality—chthonic. It is the level of ground where we plant our seeds and bury our dead. Maybe this is good ground for personal growth, rather than the kind that is full of intention and from where we can see what is going on.

As events come and go, as we read and experience and learn, all this material metamorphoses into bits of images and becomes the imagination, which is the bedrock of personality. But for the imagination to flourish, we may have to surrender, as do artists of all kinds, to a looser life and a more liberated imagination. We may have to say words and make things while not knowing what is going on. We may have to become somebody we never intended to be. We may have to let life happen in a way that challenges our plans, our values, and our hopes.

Whenever I stand in the presence of a powerful, creative person I feel the impact of the deep spirit responsible for that person's life and personality, and I am aware that even this person may not know anything of this other presence. I may see it more clearly because I am touched and pressed by its palpability. It is this deep force of vitality, not intention and by all means not consciousness, that grants personality. In fact, a certain self-forgetfulness may be just the item that allows the soul to break through with forcefulness and creativity.

D‌ISCOVERING WITH UNLIMITED EMPATHY THE WAYS PEOPLE ARE
HUMAN, WE BECOME THE PERSON WE WOULD HOPE TO BE.

In my early thirties I discovered the writings of James Hillman. At that time his major books had yet to be published, and so I collected essays he was publishing in Europe. Soon we began a correspondence, and then we met and unexpectedly became neighbors. I spent several years reading and rereading his writings and those of his colleagues. They were forming something called "archetypal psychology," which turned out not to be a school or movement or system. Later, each of those originating and brilliant psychologists went their own way, fulfilling the core idea of archetypal psychology—to allow the soul to show itself so compellingly that a strong individual life emerges. Today archetypal psychology seems to be a thing of the past, a short-lived inspiration that appeared as a seed and quickly sank back into the earth. Because of this honest, organic quality, I trust it even more than when I was an active participant and it was flourishing.

One reason I appreciated archetypal psychology was the intense interest its creators showed toward the many ways human life takes shape. I learned from these thoughtful people to appreciate both oddity and real shadow in the showings of the soul. If a therapy client was acting in a bizarre fashion, we didn't indulge in any personal revulsion or take a high moral road or psychologically try to force the person to fit more neatly into polite society. Actively and open-mindedly we wondered what was going on. We asked the key archetypal question: What does the soul want?

Many years after our initial programs, lectures, and writings, which spelled out the peculiarities of archetypal psychology, James Hillman and I found ourselves on a stage in the American Midwest giving a two-day seminar. We read poetry to each other, talked about the processes of writing and the notion of inspiration, and disagreed over a few interpretations. For example, I simply don't feel like a disciplined person, even though I get books written and keep studying the classics. My sense of my work is not one of discipline. James believed differently, and I could tell from the looks he gave me that he didn't trust my self-analysis. That is fine, because one thing I learned as a therapist was how oddly people understand themselves and how often their reading of themselves seems far off the mark.

That weekend, as part of the seminar, each of us read from a work in progress. I read passages from my book on sex, in particular the sections on classical gestures of Aphrodite. James read his speech on Shakespeare, which he had given as part of the celebrations opening the new Globe Theatre in London. I was entranced by his powerful reflections and interpretations, bold and original as usual, but I also thought about this singular quality that attracted me in archetypal psychology: a profound, genuine fascination for the deep ways human life takes form.

As Mark Van Doren, the great teacher at Columbia University, says about

Shakespeare in true Platonic fashion: "Those lines of his stun us because they are perfect statements of what we already know."[24] Both Shakespeare and archetypal psychology take their power from their capacity to reveal what we all know, if we were only to think openly enough, about the fundamentals of human life. If we could live from that deep place of recognition, we might allow ourselves the beauty of our eccentricity and tolerate in others their efforts to find their souls in the odd collection of emotions, fantasies, and behaviors that form the raw material of a human life.

At night in my bed I longed
for my only love.
I sought him but did not find him.
The Song of Songs²⁵

Oᴜʀ ᴅᴇᴇᴘ ʜᴜᴍᴀɴ sᴇxᴜᴀʟɪᴛʏ ᴡɪʟʟ ʙᴇ ꜰᴜʟꜰɪʟʟᴇᴅ ᴏɴʟʏ ᴡʜᴇɴ ᴡᴇ ᴅɪsᴄᴏᴠᴇʀ ᴛʜᴀᴛ ᴛʜᴇ ʟᴏᴠᴇʀ ᴡᴇ sᴇᴇᴋ ɪs ᴅɪᴠɪɴᴇ ᴀɴᴅ ʙᴇʏᴏɴᴅ ꜰɪɴᴅɪɴɢ.

People are often frustrated when they discover that their deepest longing never goes away. They get married and eventually fantasize about another partner. They move to a lovely place and soon wish they could be elsewhere. They love their children but wish they were closer to the ideal children they once hoped for. They have the money, the career, and the home they always wanted, and yet this isn't enough to quell the motor of desire that hums incessantly somewhere beneath the heart.

Desire is the proper atmosphere of the sexual kingdom. It keeps us alive and moving along. It keeps us in touch with memories, warm and sad, and it allows us entry to the world of imagination when all around us practicality is insistent. From the viewpoint of the soul, desire simply is; it need not be satisfied. Desires are also contained one within another, like little fish in big fish, like a Russian egg that holds a Russian egg that holds a Russian egg.

The little desires are connected to and call forth the bigger ones. Longing for chocolate might be a small desire that resides in the larger one that yearns for the sweet life. And so every desire is worth paying attention to, even though we know that if we track it far enough, we will discover that this longing will never cease. But that is the definition of divinity from the viewpoint of sexuality. That full, bittersweet, empty feeling is like incense in a church—it announces the presence of God.

If we believe the poet who wrote the Song of Songs, the divine is to be sought in our bed, at night. Sexuality certainly brings people together and makes life feel full and vital. But it is also the path toward that extreme of desire, that ultimate love that usually feels unrequited, which is the eternal and the infinite. The opening made by desire, that hole in our satisfaction, is the opening to divinity, and only there is our desire brought into the realm of the possible.

Sex is never a purely physical act. It is always numinous, even when it is not perfect or is full of shadow. In rape, the soul is savaged, not just the body. Rape and other forms of sexual abuse are sacrileges because the body is truly a manifestation of the soul and is in a real sense a temple of liminality where the divine and the human engage in many forms of intercourse. Sex abuse is a signal that we are trying hard to keep the divine out of our desire.

The bed, then, is a ritual object, worthy of our tenderest care. It has often been said that one of the most intimate sights is a bed recently left, its coverings scattered and laid about. In bed, we leave the plane of practicality and enter the deep worlds of dream, and here we make love, and in so doing we seek him whom we love but can never find. The bed is a prie-dieu on which we lie rather than kneel, a place of physical prayer, inspired by desire and sustained by pleasure. No altar is more sacred.

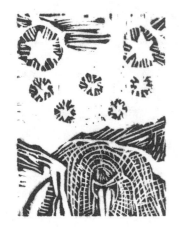

The last temptation is the greatest treason:
To do the right deed for the wrong reason.

T. S. Eliot[26]

Imagination is more weighty than fact.

It is difficult for a modern person, influenced by the myth of fact so embedded in our thoughts and values, to realize the importance of imagination. We are educated to prove our intuitions with empirical experiments and studies. Anything not verifiable by investigation of the senses we consider suspicious at best.

This materialistic view of things gives us a half-life, a partial view of experience. The images of memory, dream, and fantasy then become useless, if not interfering. We distrust intuition and imagination as superstitious, a charge that quickly wounds our modern notion of intelligence. These other powers make us feel inferior, and we can't wait until our suppositions are proven by some sort of hardware or research design.

Closely related to justifying imagination with proof is the idea that anything worthwhile is practical and applicable to our life situation. Recently, for example, it has become popular to dismiss the writings of Sigmund Freud and his followers on the basis of their clinical invalidity. If they work in practice, they are acceptable. If they are shown to be ineffective clinically, then toss them out.

Yet the Freudians have deepened our reflection on human experience. Like a work crew making a hole through a mountain, they have blasted out a portion of the interior life. Their writings are still fruitful for helping us see the subtle innuendos of the most ordinary events. Whether or not they are clinically effective depends a great deal on the clinician's fantasy of health and positive outcome.

In other words, the myth of fact has invaded the world of psychology as well, where we use a half-brained approach that esteems behavior and ignores meaning, except where meaning might offer some degree of behavioral change. In this scenario meaning itself becomes unreal, a matter for the philosphers but not the hard-core practitioners.

As a result of these biases and the half-thoughts that pass for whole ideas, we are a population that is satisfied with sound-bite news, instant and opinionated political analysis, manipulative popular psychology, and insubstantial novels and magazines. At the same time, and understandably, we feel the absence of meaning and are speechless when we learn of atrocities in our society. We don't know how to think about them because we don't know how to think, and we don't know how to think because we don't believe that thinking for its own sake is worthy of our attention. We educate our children to make a good living rather than to become thinking persons, and often we honor as celebrities those who have not made a genuine contribution to society but who mirror our own madness.

This half-life existence, where imagination and ideas are ignored, comes from a surrender to a purely physical and literal understanding of events. In the currently accepted view, as long as you do the right thing, it makes little difference what your reason is. But this, says T. S. Eliot, is the greatest treason, a betrayal of our humanity, because the interior life counts. Without it we are indeed machines that can be manipulated genetically and given new mechanical parts. In this half-life there is no hope for immortality of any kind because only the current situation is real. In this half-life there is nothing of weighty and enduring interest, because the soul is ignored as uproven—the very thing that gives life ultimate value and makes it all worth living.

We all move on the fringes of eternity and are
sometimes granted vistas through the fabric of illusion.
Ansel Adams[27]

THE VEIL THAT RENDERS LIFE OPAQUE IS INFINITESIMALLY THIN AND
CAN BE REMOVED WITH THE MERE BREATH OF IMAGINATION.

Many of us are looking far and wide for the spirit. We forget, even the most
spiritually sophisticated, that it is closer to us than we are to ourselves. The
thinnest membrane of dogged pragmatism and literalism keeps it hidden from
us. We are blind to it, as the ancient master said, because of the sheer vapor of
a cloud of unknowing. A moment's preoccupation with the so-called real world
sends the world's soul into hiding, giving the illusion that it is not present at all
or that it doesn't even exist.

As we deal with life day after day, hour after hour, in practical terms, taking
it only at face value, we ourselves become rigid, thick, and opaque. Our language becomes one-dimensional, our personalities flat. We say what we mean,
and only what we mean. Shallow slogans and opinions, picked up from the

media and from conversation, pour out of us as though we were mere recording machines. The deep soul that gives us vitality and interesting substance goes so far into hiding that it becomes invisible.

The way to wake up to vitality is first to find holes in the illusory literalism of everyday life. Ansel Adams used a camera to see through the film that covers over the world's lively personality. Others use oils on canvas or crafted words on paper. The skin of literalism can be penetrated, but some kind of technique is required—an art, a craft, a rite. The camera lens can do it, when the eye of the photographer is penetrating. A mirror might do, if we could get past the literal reflections to the wonder inspired by reflected images.

The key to seeing the world's soul, and in the process wakening one's own, is to get over the confusion by which we think that fact is real and imagination an illusion. It is the other way around. Fact is an illusion, because every fact is part of a story and is riddled with imagination. Imagination is real because every perception of the world around us is absolutely colored by the narrative or image-filled lens through which we perceive. We are all poets and artists as we live our daily lives, whether or not we recognize this role and whether or not we believe it.

It is possible to live artfully in life's constant stream of poetry. We can be educated in imagination by the arts, and that is why the arts are primary in any soul-focused education. In the arts we see the images, the stories and pieces of story that give meaning and value to the most ordinary details of a life. A still life reveals the soul in a kitchen. A landscape teaches us that nature has a personality. A sonata recapitulates the rhythms and moving forms of experience.

Once we penetrate the illusory veil of literalism and glimpse the layers in events, we may never go back to the fabrications of fact. We will have become poets of the everyday. The writer sees a flash of sense in reality and with his art keeps that vision at hand. In this sense we are all called to be poets. We can always hear further reverberations of significance in everything that happens and in all that is. We can always sound that resonance in the way we shape our lives and do our work.

The pulse of life is as close as our own throbbing veins, but everything around us conspires to convince us of its nonexistence and unworthiness. The poet and the artist have no place in a society that has forgotten the soul. But we can live differently, basking in the exoticism and eccentricity of a life of vision. The camera of our awakening may be Iris, the messenger sprite, our own eyes of the imaginal that look at the flat of existence and see the poetry.

*The quality of the imagination
is to flow, and not to freeze.*
Ralph Waldo Emerson[28]

THINKING THAT IS ALIVE NEVER STOPS TO ADMIRE ITSELF.

Many people are aware that to stay healthy the body needs exercise and movement, but few recognize that it is equally important to keep one's thinking in motion. So often we are satisfied with ideas we picked up years ago and have kept locked up for decades. Our way of looking at the world remains fixed, even as everything in life changes from minute to minute.

Of course ancient ideas and insights are of inestimable value, but even they need constant revisioning lest they become rigid. During the European Renaissance it was thought that the first role of the imagination was to keep old thoughts fresh through reflection, interpretation, and re-presentation. Why listen to yet another performance of Beethoven's *Seventh Symphony* unless there is new life in the phrasing or in the dynamics? Life itself can be interpreted, the way an imaginative performer gives life to an old masterpiece. We don't have to do anything the way it has always been done.

There are two ways of being: kinetic and static. Something in us wants to venture outward, explore, discover, reinvent. Something else wants to enjoy what has been achieved—protect, conserve, be still. In the best of circumstances, both principles have their influence, and so we explore and go home, discover and maintain, reinvent and don't change a thing. But life is rarely so balanced; instead, we become persons dedicated either to adventure or to the status quo.

Kinetic people burn out quickly and often live brief lives. The spiritual writer Alan Watts, who entitled his autobiography *In My Own Way,* was one such adventurer. Shortly after Watts died, I asked a friend of his about his life. "He burned and burned and finally went up in smoke," the friend said. Others said that the main flow in his life was alcohol. In his memoirs he tells of peeing contests he engaged in—one of the many ways streams played a part in his life and philosophy. In his journal, Watts wrote about standing in a brook on Mount Tamalpais: "I, too, am in flow and likewise have no final destination."[29] Everything Watts touched, from Zen teaching to clothing to way of life, he made alive and his own. And in his feverish reinventing of the spiritual life, he kept the traditions present and vibrant.

I find myself kinetic in my imagination and static in external things. I imagine that I will travel around the world. I go on trips, but the truth is I have not taken many real journeys, which are different from working trips. I do very little from day to day and consider a perfect time a day with nothing on the calendar. I love Monday mornings, the time we wash our clothes and write our books. Yet I sail in imagination and like to leave nothing I touch uncontaminated by my own fleeting ways of thinking.

I have seen this pattern in my father: the older he gets, the more lively his imagination becomes. He seems younger than ever, and yet he is in his mid-eighties. Nothing for him is frozen, nothing beyond reinvention, and yet he remains happy in his sixty-year marriage, his lifelong habit of collecting stamps, and his equally long devotion to the Catholic way of life. I see it in my mother, whose strong faith and generous heart intensify with age.

In the intersection of movement and stasis, life becomes interesting and is worth living. Change ennobles tradition, and honoring the old gives grounding to vitality and movement. The waters of a mountain stream flow constantly and yet it is one stream, a static picture of endless flow.

Religion without sex is a rattling skeleton,
and sex without religion is a mass of mush.
Alan Watts[10]

S EX AND RELIGION ARE CLOSER TO EACH OTHER
THAN EITHER MIGHT PREFER.

If you have ever felt awe in nature or in a church and sensed the electric atmosphere that charges the holiest moments and the most sacred places, then you
are acquainted with the numinous. Walking down the nave of a Gothic cathedral, you may feel overwhelmed by the total effect of vertical space, color,
image, sound, and atmosphere. You know that you are in the embrace of the
holy, and you perceive that holiness with your senses, not with your mind. At
its best, religion is a physical sensation.

Sex, too, is numinous. It is obviously physical, perhaps less obviously spiritual. Its power is overwhelming, and it goes beyond our attempt to understand
or control it. It has its own kind of transcendence, which takes us beyond our-

selves, and in that has much in common with religion. Sometimes it is difficult to draw the line between sex and the spiritual.

Like religion, sex brings us into the ambience of life's basic mysteries—love, marriage, and the making of children. As we try to sort out our sexuality, simultaneously we move toward meaning, values, and vision. Sex makes a life, not only physically, but spiritually. Responding to its strong drives and ardent imagination, we build our families and our homes. Our sexuality is eternally procreative.

Like sex, religion lies at the very base of experience and shapes the way we think about ourselves and our world. In religion, as in sex, we ask: Where do I come from? What is it all about? Where is it taking me? In both areas we become fired up with desire and longing and become attached to the object of our fantasy, which is typically exalted. We may imagine our relationship with the divine, as mystics of many traditions do, in the imagery of love and sexuality, and conversely we may use the language of religion to express our feelings of pleasure. The quotation from Alan Watts comes from a book on the erotic temples of India, where religion and sexuality are so graphically united that they are a scandal to some and a great enticement to others.

Official religion generally reacts to sex with moral concern. I grew up thinking that the only real sin was sex, and that almost anything having to do with sex was morally wrong. Nothing could be further from the image of religion I grew up with than a temple surrounded by images of men and women in various postures of lovemaking. This incongruence is sharper than any blending of church with warfare or money.

Such a strong moral concern on the part of religion must betray an intense involvement with sex, even as the church tries to keep sex within bounds. The moralism in religion's preoccupation with sex covers over intense interest.

Religion and sex are like a brother and sister who don't want to show their love for each other and instead fight and compete. Their love may be hidden, but its concealment is a further sign of its intensity.

If we were to see through the games religion plays with sex, we might find significant measures of spirituality in our sexuality and sexual delights in our religion. We might discover that they are two sides of a coin, one defended against by making it excessively spiritual and the other by imagining it as purely physical.

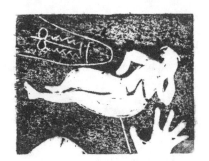

The daimonic was manifested
only in contradictions.
Goethe[31]

Bᴇᴛᴡᴇᴇɴ ᴛʜᴇ ᴛᴡᴏ ᴘʀᴇꜱꜱᴜʀᴇꜱ ᴏꜰ ᴘᴀꜱꜱɪᴏɴ
ᴀɴᴅ ɪᴅᴇɴᴛɪᴛʏ ᴡᴇ ᴄʀᴇᴀᴛᴇ ᴀ ʟɪꜰᴇ.

The Greeks used the word *daimon* as a general description of a nameless god or goddess, a spirit that could be powerful but that didn't have an elaborate story or a clear identity. In the *Iliad* we see the daimon warning and advising the soldiers as they go about their dangerous work, making decisions of life and death. Yeats emphasizes the contrast of wills between a person or group and its inspiring daimon, and he seems to do so more from experience than idea.

In modern times we seem to have lost the knack of identifying the invisible spirits that account for behavior and emotion. We know that depression, for example, can settle heavily on us, and we can understand how it might drive someone to despair and even suicide, yet we ignore the spirit as such and deal only with its physical analogue. We consider it naive to speak as though invisible presences were real.

Along with the disappearance of the daimon in our worldview, which is a kind of death of God, we have also lost the habit of learning about the daimon in stories. Once, people became acquainted with the spirits that affect human life through powerful tales. But today we sit vacantly in front of a television or movie screen and see the shells of those sacred stories, shaped according to formula and given the ending voted most pleasing by patrons. We avert its antithetical quality, but though we have forgotten the daimonic, it is real and hasn't gone away.

We are still driven by daimons, but we give them abstract names—power, greed, ambition, desire, love, will. In each of these a powerful daimon resides, but we prefer to imagine the spirit euphemistically and apotropaically as psychological. As an abstraction and a problem, it can be dealt with intellectually. But the mind is not up to such a presence, which pummels and seduces us in the areas of emotion and meaning.

A daimon is not a problem; it is the source of our creativity and identity. In the daimonic it is not easy to distinguish the good and the bad. If in our fear and confusion we fail to engage it, it becomes difficult to handle, and then the negative qualities appear to dominate. But when we take on this daimonic force courageously—it does call for stoutheartedness—then we may discover how creative and constructive it can be. In a second it can spark into life a job or a romance that we have been laboring for months or years to achieve.

When we have no ongoing relationship to the daimon, it metamorphoses into a demon. Because we are so attached to our limited conscious view of the nature of things, we may wrongly confuse the daimonic generally with the demonic. On the other hand, the daimonic force could be transformed into a passion for peace and a drive toward happiness; it doesn't have to be militant and negative. It demands that we adjust to it, that we constantly reimagine ourselves and our lives in relation to its creative work. It asks us to be the putty to its shaping fingers.

We might notice how our passions seem to move in a direction opposite the image we have of ourselves. This is as it should be because the self that we construct carefully in family and society may be too full of ego, conscious will, and intention to make a real life. A human being cannot manufacture a living, creative self, because only the soul is sufficiently deep and powerful and has adequate resources to give life to a personality. And the daimon is to the soul what the ego is to the self.

Surely Christ's parables have some affinity with the fables of the ancients.

Erasmus[12]

Modern life and thought have been severely weakened by a chauvinistic attitude toward paganism.

Pagan religion is the great shadow of Western culture. For almost two millennia we have identified with a monotheistic world philosophy. It isn't simply that we have favored a Judeo-Christian religious life, but that all of our institutions and our individual way of life have been developed precisely to exclude the religious piety of our pagan ancestors. Paganism is not a belief system; it is a way of life in which one appreciates the holiness of every facet of experience and honors that holiness with specific rites and images.

Pagans saw sacredness and depth everywhere, telling the stories of gods, goddesses, and other spirits whose role it was to maintain the vitality in ordinary life. They had a goddess of sexuality and a god of commerce, a god of medicine and a goddess of the pristine forest. They honored unnamed gods, and to every thing and every act they built a shrine. This making holy of every-thing in sight we call superstition and consider naive, but our sophistication, rooted in a deep rift between spirit and matter, is itself suspicious. How strange to assume that there is nothing but what can be perceived by the senses and measured in the language of quantification. What a deadening reduction to do away with the entire realm of spirit in the name of control and understanding!

When I was growing up a Catholic, we were told that we Catholics had the truth and needed to convert the poor pagan souls to our way of seeing things. Just recently I wrote an essay on the virtues of pagan spirituality, and I received letters from Christian pastors telling me how wrong I was and how dangerous it is to speak on behalf of paganism. Ours is supposedly an age of ecumenism, but apparently our largesse doesn't extend as far as pagan piety.

Without the insights of pagan spirituality, we divide our lives into two sep-arate categories—the sacred and the profane. The first is given over to the church, the second to the rest of existence. We talk about how our religious practice should influence our daily lives, but it does so at a distance because the two are imagined as fundamentally different. Our lives would be radically transformed if we could perceive, in good pagan fashion, religious issues in business, for example, and spirituality in our sexual relationships.

We are pleased with some of the achievements of the ancient Egyptian, Greek, and Roman cultures. We still benefit from their inventions in logic, language, and law, but we stop short of their theological insights. We love the practicality of Aristotle, even if his influence on our work is only implicit, but we don't know what to make of the mysticism and poetics, the focus on soul and the therapeutic life, in Plato and Plotinus.

A few theologians, such as Hugo Rahner and David Miller, have explored some of the ways pagan spiritual insight lies behind Judeo-Christian motifs and beliefs. They demonstrate that our frontal beliefs still lie on the ground of a worldly spirituality. The Celtic world, too, still shows evidence of an implicit blending of pagan and Christian. Paganism still lives, but as some say, it now thrives in the arts, and maybe that is why the most unpagan among us chastise the arts.

We are so accustomed to imagining spirituality without body, sex, and imagination that when we see them linked, we judge them spurious and treat them as a threat. For too long we have lived in the gray antipagan world of abstraction, where our God has fallen out of love with his creation. We have become too acquainted with self-restraint, so that we don't know the holiness of indulgence. When acknowledging the spirit, we look up into the emptiness of space, whereas once the pious pagan gazed down at the earth, full of animals, trees, and rivers, to make sacrifices and offer prayers.

The word *sacrifice* means "to make holy." Indeed, we would have to sacrifice something precious to reinstate pagan sensibility, but then we would have restored to us our world and our souls.

God cannot be shaken out nor strained
through a sieve by human argument.
Hildegard of Bingen[33]

WHEN WE OPEN OURSELVES TO AN INTUITION OF DIVINE MYSTERY, UNEXPECTEDLY WE FIND OUR HUMANITY.

One of the things I like about a genuine Zen master like Shunryu Suzuki is his capacity to relax, be comfortable with his life, and laugh at himself. "If we become too serious," he says, "we will lose our way. If we are playing games we will lose our way." The real spiritual teacher has come to terms with the brevity of life, its dogged imperfection, and the wispiness of happiness.

On the other hand, the typical modern person suffers from the need to know and control everything. He tries to find direct and indirect ways to outsmart his own mortality. He takes himself and his efforts with utmost seriousness, and his laughter is too often cynical and at the expense of those he exploits for his own sense of security. We moderns are driven to understand as much as possible, and that drivenness—we call it stress—we know is killing us. Like Adam, we feel compelled to choose the fruit of the tree of knowledge instead of the bliss of Edenic ignorance.

Our age is Promethean. Beneath our attempts to explore and analyze the whole of life is the wish to be immortal and all-knowing. The fire of the gods, which we have stolen, flickers in the glow of computer and television screens and blinds us in the brilliance of a rocket blasting off or a nuclear bomb exploding. We believe ourselves to be evolved, better than our ancestors and certainly more knowledgeable. We trust that our motives are generally humanitarian, even though our century has been riddled with atrocity and corruption and shows signs of barbarity unequalled in the past.

We call this self-sufficiency enlightenment, after our eighteenth-century fathers, but it is becoming gradually clearer—at least felt if not understood—that the implied repression of passion and the closing off to mystery leave us vulnerable to madness and its acting out. The age of modern enlightenment coincides with the age of increased cold, distant cruelty in war and injustice. God or divinity cannot find a way through the sieve of our certainties.

Is it possible that with the demise of belief in God we suffer the loss of human empathy and conscience? Do religion and human fulfillment go hand in hand? Is enlightenment after all antihumanitarian? The human soul is half eternal, the Renaissance philosopher says. If we ignore that half, we are only half human, and half human is almost as bad as not human at all.

Therefore, in a profound way the solution to our community problems, which we call social conflict, lies not in better understanding and better programs of repair and improvement, but in the depth and sublimity of our thoughts and affections, in deeper living and holier values. Religion as a way of life and an attitude of fundamental reverence is the only ground on which our humanity can stand and thrive—not religion as a defensive structure of anxious beliefs, but religion as an open heart capable of allowing life to unfold and strong enough to support a radical philosophy of love.

(Kadmos and Tiresias, two distinguished old men
out for the night dressed as women):
"We're two sane men in a mad city."
Euripedes[34]

THE NEED TO BE NORMAL IS THE PREDOMINANT ANXIETY
DISORDER IN MODERN LIFE.

During my college years, a popular movie shown frequently in art houses off campus was *King of Hearts*, in which Alan Bates plays a soldier who comes upon a town from which the citizens have fled, where the doors of the local asylum have been left open. The inmates, all of them quite lunatic, run the town with civility, good humor, and tender care. Their behavior is in strong contrast to that of the normal citizens and especially the soldiers, who line up a few feet from each other and shoot each other down.

Admittedly the movie is sentimental about insanity, but the idea is a good one. We tend to be maniacal about enforcing normal behavior. As a therapist I was frequently asked, "Do you know other people who have the same thoughts, fantasies, feelings?" I could see the anxiety in the questioner's eyes, and the relief if I answered, "Yes, I've come across this kind of thing many times." If I were to say, "No, I've never seen such a thing," the nervous person would doubtless have sunk deeper into neurosis.

I imagine the soul as a deep underground pool. Every day it floats up desires, ideas, and daydreams that offer new possibilities. If dreams are any indication of the material to be found in the pool, the stuff of life far transcends our notions of what is appropriate, fits our plans, or conforms to the ordered life we wish to live. To be alive means to go against the death principle that rules so many of our judgments and actions. We want order and propriety, while the vitality bubbling up from the pool bursts the seams of all notions of what is normal and proper.

When they decided to go out for the night revels dressed as women, Kadmos and Tiresias were under the influence of Dionysus. This Dionysus has been celebrated for eons as the reconciliation of any opposites representing life and death. To be unconventionally alive and willingly to let the self unravel or the ego die for the sake of vitality is Dionysian. In him there is no male or female, but rather the whole range of gender possibilities, indeed the whole gamut of life available to the imagination.

Who, then, is insane: the person who sacrifices deep desire for the sake of propriety and respectability or the one who risks disapproval in the name of vitality? Is anxiety around being normal simply the impetus needed to be well adjusted or is it truly a disorder, a disturbance of soul that limits the possibilities of life and is ultimately a form of repression?

We must be careful not to sentimentalize abnormality. Psychological disorder is usually painful and debilitating. Let us not glorify antisocial behavior. Civility allows us to survive and to thrive. The problem is not the wish to be normal, but rather the literalization of that idea. We need to adjust to the world around us, just as we need to live our eccentric selves. The wish to be normal conceals a deeper desire: negatively, an attempt to avoid the weight of our individuality, and positively, the ideal of being fully ourselves in a community where we can belong and participate.

Not only in ideas but also in action we might embrace the outrageous in our normal personal lives. Socially, we might give adequate space and recognition to times of carnival, periods of breakdown, and moments of experiment. When we make and enforce our laws, we might take care to include some tolerance of madness and generally be cautious lest we make too rational a society, where in reaction the soul shows itself only in outrageous extremes.

Not only can you analyze your unconscious,
but you can also let the unconscious analyze you.
C. G. Jung[35]

C ARE OF THE SOUL OFTEN MEANS GETTING OUT OF THE
WAY RATHER THAN DOING SOMETHING.

It is not unusual to hear someone say, "I don't know what I'm doing, but at least I'm doing something." We believe in action. Ours is a culture of doing rather than waiting, allowing, or just being. But there is a hint of secularism in the emphasis on doing, as we depend on our own resources rather than relying on something beyond ourselves. Religion recommends some degree of acquiescence and searching for extra-human help, but the modern person may find such an attitude weak and even masochistic. This may be one reason why religion is not as strong as it used to be. Maybe, too, this is why many people today prefer spirituality, where there may be more doing than being, over religion.

Religious teaching often goes further: it asks us not only not to do, but to be done to. In religious language this may mean letting grace pour in or allowing

God's will to be done. Psychologically we might say: be influenced, allow change, let life happen. Many people say they want to change, and their way of putting it is exactly right: they want to make the changes that they prefer, and they want to do them in their own way. But real change of heart may move in a direction counter to our will and intelligence. We can't always imagine the best way to change or predict the best outcome.

A Sufi story tells of a man who was riding a donkey up a mountain. A thief came and forced him to carry the animal up the steep slope. The man, who was a dervish, said, "God, I praise you, but sometimes you get it backward." In fact, from the divine point of view, the truth of things is often backward, and spiritual wisdom often contradicts secular prudence. If we could reverse the dictates of conventional wisdom, we might see an opening to the englargement of our souls.

As a therapist, I often followed a simple rule of thumb. I would listen to a man or woman passionately explain what was going on in their lives and what they needed to do. This strong expression of self-understanding and intention told me a great deal about their suffering. I could see where and how they were defending themselves against life. To get a glimpse of an effective way through and out of their problems, I just had to reverse their strongly held opinions. I don't mean that I literally recommended an opposite strategy or that I took a cynical attitude toward their attempts to understand. But it always seemed fruitful to explore the direction closed off by insistent plans for improving life.

To free our souls, we may have to be loosened by our suffering and our problems. Rather than look for ways to be further in control, we may have to surrender to the vitality that is trying to get some representation. Rather than understand our dreams, we might be understood by them—reimagine our lives through their challenging images. Rather than get life together, we might allow life to have its way with us and get us together in a form that is a surprise.

True personal strength is not to be found in an iron will or in superior intelligence. Real strength of character shows itself in a willingness to let life sweep over us and burrow its way into us. Courage appears as we open ourselves to the natural alchemy of personal transformation, not when we close ourselves by making the changes we think are best.

THE MEANING OF LIFE CAN BE FOUND AT ANY MOMENT WITHOUT
MOVING OUR EYES AND WITHOUT DOING ANYTHING DIFFERENTLY.

It is a mistake to think of psychotherapy as the arena in which people change. When people say they want to change, I hear a subtle rejection of the person they are. I suppose that at some level change is necessary—when life is tormenting, when one feels neurotic or psychotic, when a marriage is suffocating, when a job doesn't pay anything to the emotions. But even then, a conscious plan for change usually comes from the same imagination that got us into trouble in the first place. A new project of self-transformation may land us back in the uncomfortable wallowing hole we just left.

When people talk about finding meaning in life, they imply that they can figure things out and set them right. But meaning that makes life worth living may be nothing more than a moment's realization, a sensation, such as the touch of your baby's skin, or a sudden breathtaking appreciation for your home, or the passing thrill when you are reminded of your love for your spouse. Meaning may be an epiphany rather than an understanding.

Thinking is of immense importance, and we might have a better world if we all learned how to think. But at the same time, thinking may be only the prelude to meaning. We read, take classes, converse, study, and perhaps write. These intellectual activities are priceless, but their value may be to prepare us for an instant's recognition of the vital seed, what the ancients called the scintilla, the spark, that gives life to everything we do and see. Once we glimpse that spark, we will have learned that there is indeed a beyond that can be found in what is closest at hand. All our education might be brought to a point where it allows us to glimpse in wonder the slightest breath of life in front of us.

My piano is a universe. Those eighty-eight keys arrange the seven planets in musical scales, an aural cosmos. For some people, their garden is Eden. There they find the precious work that ushers them into eternity, where time seems to stand still and work is once again pleasure. Our homes can always point to a beyond—the eternal home where we find settling and ease. Looking through a window is never only the literal act of seeing what is outside the house; it is always, too, a ritual act, in which we look from the frame of our present circumstances out into a universe that holds the secret of our existence.

We can make our homes a world in miniature by creating a small library, if only of three books; hanging a painting or two on the wall—our own art gallery; carving or painting a sun, moon, or stars somewhere on the building to make it a cosmos. We can invite the world in with our hospitality and make it a haven for wanderers and sufferers. For our children, home is the center of the cosmos, and we can do what we can to make it a true and appropriate Eden, a garden of delight.

We can make a shrine or altar in or around our home instead of asking the churches to keep chapel at a distance. We can plant a tree in lieu of a forest and tend a yard that is our terra firma. We can make housework and avocations our primary labor, and the effort of making a living secondary. The capitalist philosophy, working for a paycheck and for the comfort of stockholders, might well promote secularism and blind us to the close beyond.

We can still the yearning heart that longs for satisfaction, not by finally finding the perfect mate, the dream house, or success in the workplace, but by perceiving, perhaps for the first time, the pulse of eternity in the moment at hand and the contours of the whole in the ordinary thing currently in sight.

Even when we are negligent and slumbering on the pillow of our sins, He disturbs us from time to time, shakes us, strikes us, and does His best to wake us up by means of tribulations.

Thomas More[37]

Wₕₑₙ THINGS DON'T GO AS HOPED AND PLANNED, WE MAY READ OUR SHOCK AND DISAPPOINTMENT AS A WAKING UP TO A DEEPER DESIGN.

This lesson from Thomas More, written as he sat in his cell in the Tower of London, might sound obvious. But remember that he was an extremely intelligent, successful, and powerful attorney and judge, knighted and made Lord Chancellor. He had no time for platitudes as he tried to devise arguments to spare his life and his family. In his cell he wrote several devotional and reflective pieces, listening closely to his conscience and sorting out the array of thoughts and feelings assaulting him as he prepared himself for the most challenging decision in his life.

One bright sunny day, I approached the Tower of London with my wife and children. We had made arrangements to visit the cell where Thomas More spent his last fourteen months. An elderly yeoman opened doors for us and led us into the cell, which is hidden behind an ordinary door of a rather Victorian-looking residence. I stood there in that remarkable room—vaulted, white-washed, austere—and imagined what it was like for this good, cultured man to be apart from his beloved family and choose between his conscience and his life.

Today we don't use the language of sin, and yet we do find ourselves slumbering on the pillow of our unconsciousness. When things go wrong, immediately we look for the cause, resolve never to get caught in such straits again, and work hard at making things right. More's recommendation comes from a different point of view, one that sees trials and difficulties as the expression of a design that runs much deeper than that of the ego, with its reliance on consciousness and intention. He lived from that deeper place and enjoyed a life full of family, friends, and personal wealth. Then, painfully, he lost his life because of the depth of his reflections.

After a lifetime given to study and self-analysis, even More felt he needed further wakening. During those times in my own life when things seemed to fall apart more than they came together, and during those hours in which I sat as a therapist with people whose lives were far from their wishes and dreams, I thought of Thomas More and the extremity of his vitality and his suffering.

It may be more important to be awake than to be successful, balanced, or healthy. What does it mean to be awake? Perhaps to be living with a lively imagination, responding honestly and courageously to opportunity and avoiding the temptation to follow mere habit or collective values. It means to be an individual, in every instance manifesting the originality of who we are. This is the ultimate form of creativity—following the lead of the deep soul as we make a life.

We all fall asleep and allow life to rush by without reflection and consideration. When we are shocked into awareness by a tragedy or failure, this is the time not simply to make resolutions for the future, but to choose to live an awakened life. The Buddha was called "the awakened one." I doubt that More would have thought of himself as a Buddhist, yet both he and that much earlier sage had this in common.

To an improper view one should not resort;
And one should not be a world-augmenter.

The Dhammapada[38]

THE BASIC CONTRIBUTION ONE CAN MAKE TO ONE'S COMMUNITY IS
NOT TO ADD TO THE GENERAL UNCONSCIOUSNESS OF THE TIME.

The Buddhist *Dhammapada*, which may be translated loosely as "the means for fulfilling the laws of your nature," teaches us here a negative lesson: Do not be a person who adds to the thoughtlessness of the time. A traditional commentary says this refers to samsara, which we sometimes inadvertently picture, using imagery that is entirely in the scope of Indian philosophy, as "the rat race." The gift of our humanity lies precisely in being able to transcend the basic needs of food, shelter, clothing, and ego rewards.

In this regard, it's interesting how spiritual people often deny themselves one or all of these necessities. The monk fasts, Jesus says he is like the bird whose only home is a nest, the Sufi nun and the Hindu holy man go without clothes, and all find the means to be liberated from self-concern. These are potential means, not necessary paths, to an awakened life.

In the West, our ideal of a whole person is someone who is adjusted, creative, not destroyed by passion and addiction, and successful by some worldly standard. *The Dhammapada* suggests an alternative ideal: a person who does not cling like a magnet to collective, unconscious values. This person realizes that the satisfaction of the ego, known to us as success or self-esteem, does not offer the deep tranquillity and the liberation from craving that quintessentially we yearn for. This awake person knows that being in tune with the law of one's nature, which is not separate from the law of community and the law of the natural world, is the best definition of happiness.

Release from absorption in collective unconsciousness might begin in the knowledge that there is an alternative. The Buddha was kept within the confines of the family palace in order to spare him awareness of sickness and death. We all live in our palaces of ignorance, and so the first step away is to see the world for what it is. We can be critical of the values that parade around us as natural and unquestioned. As Thoreau recommended, we can live the examined life.

A second step might be to shape a life that is more in tune with our perceived nature, or dharma, and stand firm in our originality and eccentricity. This intense level of self-possession comes at a price, of course, for friends and associates will feel the rub of individuality when their concern is to sustain the adaptation to unconsciousness, otherwise known as normalcy. A spouse may feel threatened, unless the marriage is built profoundly on mutual dedication to each other's dharma. Sometimes happiness is misperceived precisely as unconsciousness.

A third step would be to manifest our originality, not at all for ego rewards, but as a necessary way of giving it life and substance. Values clarification theory teaches that a value is incomplete when it is merely an idea; it has to be lived consistently and usually courageously to be a real value. The simple act of showing one's deeper nature is a form of personal liberation and a generous contribution to community.

There are many more steps in this negative process of not contributing to the unconsciousness of the time. Some are called to be prophets, being annoyingly vocal in challenging collective assumptions. Some are called to be comedians, turning accepted norms inside out. Some are called to teach, and any teacher responding to the demands of dharma always teaches release from samsara in an awakened approach to the particular subject. Many are parents, who can raise their children not to be clones of the unconsciousness but alert in their own ways. These parents invite their children out of the palace of unknowing even as they give them a loving home. All of us, in our humanity, are called to rise above the rat race and enjoy our originality.

What was your original face before you were born?
Zen koan

To LIVE FROM A DEEP PLACE IS TO GO BACK OR DOWN TO
THAT ORIGIN OF YOUR LIFE THAT IS NOT IN THE LEAST
EXPLAINED BY THE AUTOBIOGRAPHICAL MYTH.

We have a dastardly tendency to make of ourselves a structural object of analysis similar to an atom or a molecule. We trace the origins of our current problems and life situations to childhood and the family. This is our current Western, but by no means universally adopted, myth of origins. We endow trauma with the creative powers of a natural tragedy or a destructive deity. Some explain the origin of current troubles by means of older myths, like the expulsion from Eden where Adam and Eve lived a mysterious existence, but we all tend to take that mythology literally or else fancifully. We don't let its full poetic power seep into our sense of self and guide our actions and our self-analysis.

The ancient Zen koan invites us to go even further, beyond myth, as we seek our origins, the source of a sense of self, and a hint of meaning. Who were we before the story of our lives? What is the originating mystery only hinted at in biography, dreams, desires, fears, and our creations? What would happen if we were to allow this original face to be manifested in everything we do? Would it not be iconoclastic, shattering every illusory structure and image we put forth? Would it not be so terrible in its beauty and its fierceness that we would begin to feel our presence?

The loss of a sense of being is the most serious side effect of the quantified, rationalized, commodified, and industrialized life we have manufactured in recent times. When people regard us now, what they see is what they get. Our original face has been covered over with biography and statistics, so deeply layered that it would require an archeology of self to rediscover our origins.

This koan inspires me to tear up my driver's license, forget my social security number, rewrite my curriculum vitae as fiction, and never answer the question "What do you do?" I feel desperate to look once again at that original face and be reminded of who and what it is all about. I seek out the magic mirror, the reflecting pool of Narcissus. Dreams seem the most reliable of signals, and yet to the biographical world they are the most suspect.

I look into the eyes of my dog, and I seem to see a face more original than my own. It is at once more expressive and less articulate. Is this what I should be? Will my original face shine through more if I say less? Is it desirable that my original face come out from hiding at all? Are these questions behind the maddening activities of those Eastern monks who run off into silence and those Western nuns who hide from the world in cloisters?

On the other hand, perhaps all we have are Joycean epiphanies, momentary revelations, instants of complete unself-consciousness when, as D. H. Lawrence imagined, the god hidden deep within the self appears passingly. Then we find, with the mystics of many traditions, that the self and the divine are separated by the thinnest of membranes, indeed a membrane of illusion.

This leads to a practical consideration. All psychological and social problems are merely the manifestation of confluences we will never appreciate unless we can think mythically and theologically. Emerson said that only the poet knows astronomy. Perhaps only in our mystical moments do we know what is really happening in our lives. Until we ask the mythic questions, the theological questions, the mystery questions, we may be analyzing our illusions and spinning webs over the face that wants to be ours.

THE WAY TO FIND A SOUL MATE IS TO BE A PERSON WITH SOUL.

Many people are desperate to find a soul mate, someone who responds to their deep image of love and intimacy. They go to great lengths to meet people, and they spend considerable time feeling achingly deprived of the joys of intimacy they imagine. Their attitude is summed up in the frequent lament: When am I going to find the person who is right for me?

This approach to love seems to reflect the narcissism of the times. When am I going to get what I need for my growth and my satisfaction? An alternative would be to give all that attention either to one's own life—developing one's talents, educating oneself in culture, and simply becoming an interesting person—or to a needy society. This crafting of a life is a positive way of preparing oneself for intimacy.

Margaret Fuller's essay "Woman in the Nineteenth Century," written in

1844, is a rare example of profound feminist reflection linked to ancient Neo-platonic teachings about the soul. Her observations apply to men as well as women, to society as well as individuals, and to our current situation as well as hers. She was sharply aware of the tendency to find the soul's vitality exclusively in relationship with another, at the cost of one's own individuality. In the same essay she wrote, "If any individual live too much in relations, so that he becomes a stranger to the resources of his own nature, he falls, after a while, into a distraction, or imbecility, from which he can only be cured by a time of isolation, which gives the renovating fountains time to rise up."

At the same time, Margaret Fuller was capable of intense and fruitful intimacy, as in her sometimes stormy yet always creative connection with Ralph Waldo Emerson. Frequently I have occasion to visit the town of Groton, Massachusetts, and each time I think about its precious citizen Margaret Fuller and recall how in many ways she reconciled opposites in her rich and tragic life. She devoted herself to her own education, to involvement in world politics, and to deep reflection on the soul. She was capable of extraordinary friendship because she was so fervently an individual moved by her passions. She was a woman of extreme imagination and courage.

Having deep friendships and soulful relationships is the result of living one's own life seriously and devotedly. Fuller added a more demanding condition: to be able to live in isolation, in celibacy. "To be fit for relations in time, souls, whether of man or woman, must be able to do without them in the spirit." Time spent alone, the experience of being a solitary, the spirit of celibacy— these, too, can be delicious to the person seeking a vital life, and they may be important elements in the establishing of a marriage or a friendship. They are part of the quest for a soul mate because first of all one must have a soul.

The capacity for solitude is a prerequisite for intimacy with another. Otherwise, it may well be that the desperate search for a partner is merely the expression of personal emptiness, and if that is the case, any relationship will be founded on weak grounds and will not satisfy the yearning for connection. The expression *soul mate* can mean a partnership in which the soul is engaged, in which one's own soul connects with another's. This is no small thing, and it reaches far deeper than the resolution of any superficial search for romance. Part of what we long for in our wish for a soul mate is intimacy with and the expression of our own soul.

Conscious myths will always turn out to be pseudo-myths.
But by the same token we cannot coerce the symbols of
former myths when their day is done.

Stanley Romaine Hopper[40]

W E ARE CREATING A NEW VISIBLE WORLD THAT REQUIRES
A FRESH APPROACH TO THE INVISIBLE WORLD WHERE LIE
THE NARRATIVES THAT SHAPE OUR LIVES.

Myth is the narrative in which we find ourselves when we become aware that
our lives are shaped by stories. The myth at work at any particular moment
may derive from the family and from powerful but hidden currents of imagination strong in the culture. Our basic humanity also accounts for the deepest
stratum of our lived myth. We are always in a myth, but cultural narratives do
vary from one place to another, and even in a single culture they can shift over
time.

Although the myths we are living are largely subterranean—we are not
much aware of their influence or even their nature—we can glimpse them and
achieve an important degree of self-awareness, where we don't feel com-

pletely compelled by the unconscious strength of the deep story. Knowing the stories that motivate us offers a significant degree of freedom.

During my graduate school years at Syracuse University I studied religion and literature with Stanley Hopper, who was a forerunner among the still small group of scholars who look to novelists, poets, and philosophers for indications about the religious life and religious dimensions of the culture. Professor Hopper's work was focused on elucidating what he saw as a major mythic shift occurring in our day.

Ours is a time, Hopper said, when the myth that has sustained us for centuries is weakening. What he meant, in part, is that our sense of the divine is no longer as externally placed as in a former time. We are now more inward in our focus, and our notion of divinity and the nature of things is changing accordingly. We are also breaking away from the dualistic world of inner and outer, mind and matter, and even fact and imagination.

In this time of deep change, we may feel dislocated and neurotically worried about our center and source of grounding. Sensing the waning of a myth, we may take several different steps: We may try to reinstate the old myth, insisting that it is the only truth that will hold us together. We may try to invent new myths, but these, Hopper says, are without sufficient depth or numinosity. They are too rational and fail to give us the deep inspiration we need. We may also turn to countermyths, stories that emphasize a vision opposite to that of the dominant but weakening myth. Our literature and movies show fragmentation, falling apart, destruction, violence, and hopelessness.

Hopper's solution for our sense of mythic vertigo is a new appreciation for the role of imagination. He recommends that we replace theology, the rationalistic interpretation of belief, with theopoetics, finding God through poetry and fiction, which neither wither before modern science nor conflict with the complexity of what we know now to be the self. This is a theology for a period highly influenced by technology and by psychoanalysis.

Hopper's theological vision is remarkably similar, as far as I can tell, to Eastern views, where we are advised to keep our ideas and narratives empty. As I understand this, it means that we can no longer approach the ultimate questions of human existence as matters of fact. We can live out our stories with great seriousness and courage, but at the same time we have to reflect on what we're doing and realize that at some level our formulations are illusory. Our theological stories may now have to be more poetic than quasifactual, as they have been. Our truth is now our myth.

If we could make this shift, which is being forced on us by our very success in science and other areas of knowledge, we might find a more solid security, one that is not easily disturbed by the findings of science or the shifting of mores. We would realize that our conceptions about the nature of things are always provisional and therefore may best be served by a poetic sensibility that looks deep into experience. Our sense of the religious life might be less external, less factual, and less rationalistic.

Stanley Hopper was a quiet man, traditional in his imagination and style. Yet his point of view is still a radical one. It offers a way to save religion from irrelevancy, and yet people who consider themselves religious might not get his point. They might see him as a threat to religion rather than its caretaker. Still, what he challenges is not faith and not a spiritual way of life, but outmoded ways of being religious. For him, faith is anchored in the wisdom of the poet rather than in the illusion of fact, which in many cases has kept religion unsophisticated and ineffective. He recommends that we let go of a decaying narrative and find meaning in the myth that is rising in its place.

THE ESSENCE OF RELIGION IS TO SEE THE SUBLIME AND
THE AWESOME IN THE LOWLIEST OF THINGS.

The greatest mystery of religion is the incarnation, the divine and the spiritual taking human and worldly form. In the early history of Christianity, several heresies arose on this point, and they are understandable. It is still difficult to appreciate how the absolutely spiritual is revealed in the absolutely ordinary and material. Our natural tendency is to seek spirituality in the thin air of abstraction rather than in the concrete life around us.

Norman O. Brown takes up an ancient tale that has captivated me for over twenty years: the story of Daphne, a wood spirit who echoes the great goddess Artemis. Artemis and her several avatars, figures of fantasy like Diana, Snow White, and Daphne, is the absolute embodiment of purity, and in particular the purity we sense in the center of an inviolate forest. Apollo, a purist in his own right, but a divine artist and healer found in the midst of culture, becomes aflame with desire for Daphne. She refuses him and flees. Maybe it is his bodilessness she most resists. Pointedly, she avoids him by becoming a tree—a fall into a lower order of creation, Brown says.

Desperate, Apollo embraces the tree, just as we purists can find the object of our devotion in the world at hand. Pure spirit, or spiritual purity, has been incarnated in wood. The musician can pick up a violin and take us to the heights of spirit. The architect can join timbers together and make a temple or a Gothic cathedral. We can find God in the home we are making daily.

As above, so below is a summary of the Emerald Tablet, an ancient spiritual manifesto that has inspired alchemists and artists for centuries. I like to think of this tablet as a green table, like a billiard table, which has long been compared to the field on which life plays itself out, complete with hazards—holes we drop into as we carom imperfectly across the green lay of our lives in our pursuit of the good life. On the green table the sublime and the ordinary find common ground. Whatever happens down here has direct implications for what is happening up there. And vice versa.

A terrible ethic follows when body and spirit are no longer divided. We had better take good care of our bodies, our homes, our children, our work, our arts, and our material world. My version of green table wisdom goes this way: The more engaged we are in the material world, the more spiritual we will be. The more spiritually awake we are, the more generously we will engage material existence. If we neglect one, the other will suffer.

According to an old tradition in both the East and the West, when a human being has crafted some object beautifully and properly, a spirit will be so enticed by it that it will take up residence in that thing. If this is true—and this is one of the firmest of my religious beliefs—then millions of objects around us are available for our spiritual benefit. But not every object qualifies, because apparently the spirits can distinguish between the genuine and the bogus.

Look around your home and decide which objects are most likely to have charmed a spirit. Which spirits dwell in your environment? Are they encouraged to remain? Which objects are of no interest to passing angels? We might define religion as the art of making and maintaining a material world of such beauty and propriety that it will be the desired home of every kind of spirit. Ancient Greek philosophers taught that the whole world is full of spirits. Can we say the same about our cities and our homes?

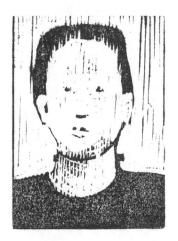

T HE WAY OUT OF THE DEHUMANIZING EFFECTS OF MODERN CAPITALISM AND INDUSTRIALISM IS NOT TO CHANGE THE SYSTEM BUT TO READ GOOD BOOKS.

Images flow through the mind without limit. Especially in moments of concentration and quiet, when we might like to have a peaceful mind, the gears of imagination gain speed. We may be flooded with family memories and then suddenly realize that we live much of our adult lives in imitation of or in rebellion against scenes and personalities of the family drama. Free-floating images may arise, and who knows where they come from, as they appear in daydreams, night dreams, waking fantasies, wishes, and fears. Everything that passes the filter of our attention becomes material for an alchemy by which raw images are transformed into a personality and a life. Images are like ants, which invisibly sustain the life that is almost always unconscious of their presence.

The images that form the raw material of our imagination are the most precious substance we have because from them we develop an attitude toward events and eventually a way of life. Education of the soul is largely a matter of creating a treasury of images and skills for dealing with them. It is as important for engineers and MBAs to read Shakespeare, a master image-maker, for this purpose as it is for the physician, the therapist, or the parent. A great deal depends on whether the books we read and the movies we see hone the imagination or make it blunt.

As Mary Shelley describes so precisely in her metaphor of the monster, we live in an age when schools and businesses stitch together the fragments of a personality and call it a human being, useful for production. But when Frankenstein's monster one day witnesses the tender emotions of a family and begins to read the great poets, he can no longer bear his monstrosity. He becomes aware of the distance between his manufactured self and his sublime possibilities.

A thread of sentimentality taints, perhaps, Mary Shelley's portrait of the commodified and industrialized person. Plutarch could be helpful, but we also need the grisly images of fairy tales, the haunting, nauseating images of Sade, Kafka, and Beckett, and the pained confessions of Plath and Sexton, so that we can reflect on evil and not just be its victims. We need the erotic images of literature and religion to keep us in tune with desire and pleasure, for without a schooled imagination, the erotic life can get out of hand and be disconnected from other necessary sensibilities.

If the books sold in airports, those named by political leaders as their favorites, and those piled high on best-seller lists are any indication, and if the movies that succeed in theaters and even the children's books put out by large companies insensitive to literature and art say something about ourselves, then we are treating our imaginations with contempt.

Yet we are what we read. We are the educators of our own personalities. Certainly we have great influence in the crafting of our children. If we brought half the intelligence to the making of souls that we bring to the making of machines, we would be people of character and imagination. We would be sharp and therefore less inclined to kill and cheat each other. We would know where to find the deep pleasures, so we would be less desperate for shallow entertainments and the ephemeral gratifications of gadgets.

In memorable B-movies Frankenstein's monster is big and stiff, and he has a highly visible, highly symbolic pipe stretching through his neck. He is us when we lose our supple grace by crowding our imaginations with what a composition teacher of mine in music school used to call, without fussy propriety, crud.

The Savior laughed and said to them:
"What are you thinking about?
[Why] are you perplexed?
What are you searching for?"
Philip said: "For the underlying reality
of the universe and the plan."
"The Sophia of Jesus Christ"[43]

DEEP TRUST AND GOOD HUMOR ARE SIGNS OF SPIRITUAL WISDOM.

I am surprised that in the sacred scriptures Jesus is rarely, if ever, shown laughing. Some of his sayings are certainly comic, and I have no doubt that a clever writer could produce a one-man show of Jesus teaching a cynical world his upside-down philosophy of love. In this passage from an early Gnostic tale, his followers interview Jesus after his resurrection. We find the devoted and serious disciples wondering about the underlying nature of the universe and its plan. Jesus laughs at their lofty questions and teaches them about holy ignorance and divine ineffability.

A certain kind of laughter erupts from a comfortable consent to the lowliness of human nature. We laugh when a child discovers some basic truth, like the principle of gravity. Many traditions show the Buddha, that figure of absolute composure in the face of pure existence, smiling or laughing. For many years I have kept on my desk a laughing Buddha who is swarming with little monks who crawl all over his ample torso. In the sacred story of Hermes, from the ancient Greeks, the child god approaches the great Zeus as his brother Apollo complains about his audacity. Zeus laughs and reconciles these two fundamental life structures—impish, unpredictable Magic and cool blue Logic.

I understand Jesus to be saying, "Why are you asking all these questions? Get on with life and have some faith." Later in this remarkable gospel Jesus describes how the world came to be and offers an alternative to bland curiosity: "Son of Man consented with Sophia, his consort, and revealed a great androgynous light. His male name is designated 'Savior, Begetter of All Things.' His female name is designated 'All-Begettress Sophia.' Some call her 'Pistis.'"

Pistis means "trust." To create a worthy life, we may have to trust rather than gain insight into the overall plan. When our faith is fragile, and we have to insist on our own beliefs at the expense of others', the comfort needed for laughter is missing. The kind of laughter modeled by Jesus, the Buddha, and Zeus is rooted in humble acknowledgment of our limitations. We laugh because we can live comfortably not knowing everything.

A few writers have pictured Jesus as a comic, a significant sign of his divinity. But the stand-up comedian and the film comic are also Christ figures. They help us get some distance from our dangerous seriousness. A person who believes too earnestly in his own convictions can be dangerous to others, for absence of humor signals a failure in basic humanity. The laughter of the holy sage is the beginning of wisdom, and wisdom, Sophia, is deep trust joined with knowledge.

Some laughter is cynical and crude, but there is another kind that expresses a simple trust in life. I have heard this laughter from many men and women of wisdom I have known over the years, and I am certain that Jesus laughed in this way as he taught. It is unfortunate that the church established to perpetuate his presence has chosen not to picture a laughing Jesus. It is an oversight that leaves the teaching unnecessarily severe and incomplete.

Life is a divine comedy, and until we discover how those two words go together, we will be condemned to spiritual depression and severity, signs that we have not yet found God and that we are layers and eons away from our original self. In the mystical land before our birth, heartfelt laughter is the signal that God is present.

Notes

1. *Zen Mind, Beginner's Mind,* ed. Trudy Dixon (New York: Weatherhill, 1973), p. 138.
2. *Faith in a Seed*, ed. Bradley P. Dean (Washington, D.C., and Covelo, Calif.: Island Press/Shearwater Books, 1993), p. 183.
3. Stephen E. Ehicher, ed. *Selections from Ralph Waldo Emerson* (Boston: Houghton Mifflin Company, 1957), p. 381.
4. *Echo's Subtle Body* (Dallas: Spring Publications, 1982), p. 95.
5. Terry Southern and Mason Hoffenberg, *Candy* (New York: Penguin Books, 1964), p. 11.
6. *Confessions*, transl. Henry Chadwick (Oxford: Oxford University Press, 1991), p. 200.
7. Richard Lattimore, transl. *The Odyssey of Homer* (New York: Harper & Row, 1967), p. 66.
8. Raymond Klibansky, Erwin Panofsky, and Fritz Saxl, *Saturn and Melancholy* (New York: Basic Books, 1964), 272, n. 102.
9. *Selected Letters*, ed. Thomas H. Johnson (Cambridge, Mass.: The Belknap Press, 1986), p. 211.
10. Thomas H. Johnson, ed. *Emily Dickinson Selected Letters* (Cambridge, Mass.: Harvard University Press, 1986), p. 208.
11. Quoted in Nancy Wilson Ross, *The World of Zen* (New York: Vintage Books, 1960), p. 260.
12. Ross, p. 258.
13. Charles Boer, ed. Ovid's *Metamorphoses I* (Dallas: Spring Publications, 1989), p. 14.
14. Anne Sexton, "Again and Again and Again," *The Complete Poems* (Houghton Mifflin, 1981), p. 196.
15. *La lunga notte dei nove sentieri* (Firenze: Quaderni di Hellas, 1981), p. 13.
16. William Butler Yeats, *Mythologies* (New York: Collier Books, 1959), p. 362.
17. Quoted in Thomas Moore, *The Planets Within* (Lewisburg, Pa.: Bucknell University Press, 1982), p. 98.

18. *Selections from Ralph Waldo Emerson*, "Circles," p. 168.

19. *The Flowing Light of the Godhead,* transl. Frank Robin (New York: Paulist Press, 1998), p. 47.

20. Anne Sexton, "Angels of the Love Affair," *The Complete Poems* (Boston: Houghton Mifflin Company, 1981), p. 332.

21. Robert Francis, "Blue Winter," *American Poet*, Fall, 1998.

22. *Emily Dickinson Selected Letters*, p. 210.

23. Warren V. Bush, ed. *The Dialogues of Archibald MacLeish and Mark Van Doren* (New York: E. P. Dutton & Co., 1964), p. 29.

24. Ibid.

25. Transl. Ariel Bloch and Chana Bloch (Berkeley: University of California Press, 1995), p. 67.

26. *Murder in the Cathedral* (New York: Harcourt, Brace & World, 1963), p. 44.

27. Ansel Adams and Mary Street Alinder, *Ansel Adams: An Autobiography* (New York: New York Graphic Society Books, Little, Brown, 1985), p. 382.

28. Carl Bode and Malcom Cowley, eds. *The Portable Emerson* (New York: Penguin Books, 1981), p. 260.

29. Monica Furlong, *Genuine Fake: A Biography of Alan Watts* (London: Unwin Hyman Limited, 1986), p. 182.

30. Alan Watts and Eliot Elisofon, *Erotic Spirituality* (New York: Collier Books, 1971), p. 80.

31. Quoted in Rollo May, *Love and Will* (New York: W. W. Norton & Company, 1969), p. 130.

32. "Letter to Martin Dorp (1514)," in Desiderius Erasmus, *The Praise of Folly*, transl. Clarence H. Miller (New Haven: Yale University Press, 1979), p. 143.

33. *The Letters of Hildegard of Bingen,* transl. Joseph L. Baird and Radd K. Ehrman (New York: Oxford University Press, 1994), p. 112.

34. *The Bakkahi*, transl. Robert Bagg (Amherst: University of Massachusetts Press, 1978), p. 26.

35. *Letters,* ed. Gerhard Adler and Aniela Jaffé, transl. R. F. C. Hull, Bollingen Series I, vol. 1 (Princeton: Princeton University Press, 1973), p. 460.

36. *Letters and Papers from Prison*, ed. Eberhard Bethge (New York: Collier Books, 1971), p. 376.

37. "De Tristitia Christi," quoted in Alistair Fox, *Thomas More: History and Providence* (New Haven: Yale University Press, 1982), p. 247.

38. *Sacred Writings: The Dhammapada*, transl. John Ross Carter and Mahinda Palihawadana (New York: Oxford University Press, 1987), p. 232.

39. Mary Kelley, ed. *The Portable Margaret Fuller* (New York: Penguin Books, 1994), p. 295.

40. "Myth, Dream, and Imagination," in *Myths, Dreams, and Religion*, ed. Joseph Campbell (New York: E. P. Dutton & Co., 1970), p. 118.

41. "Daphne, or Metamorphosis," in *Myths, Dreams, and Religion*, ed. Joseph Campbell (New York: E. P. Dutton & Co., 1970), p. 99.

42. Mary Shelley, *Frankenstein* (New York: Modern Library, 1984), p. 137.

43. James M. Robinson, ed. *The Nag Hammadi Library,* transl. Douglas M. Parrott, rev. ed. (San Francisco: HarperSanFrancisco, 1988), p. 222.